The Art of June Wayne

December 5, 1998 –
for Bonnie with
kind regards,

June Wayne

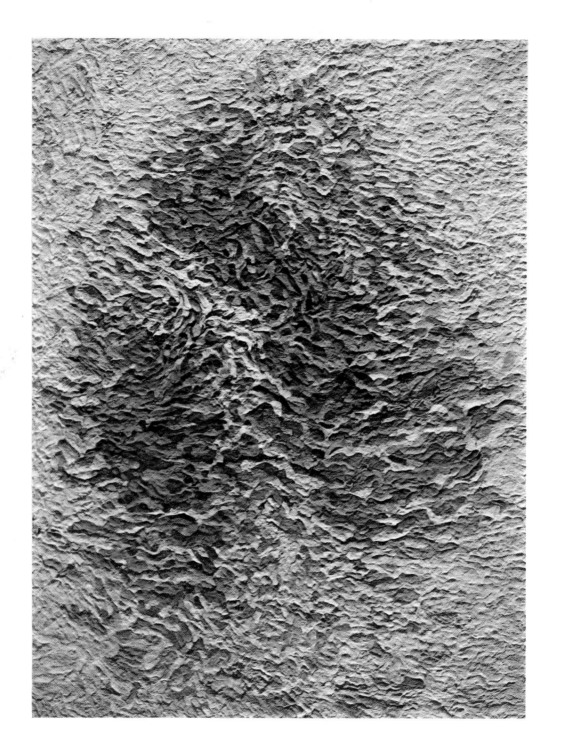

THE ART OF JUNE WAYNE

by Mary W. Baskett · Curator of Prints

Cincinnati Art Museum

Harry N. Abrams, Inc., New York

Gebr. Mann Verlag Berlin

FRONTISPIECE: Sixti-Sexate, September 20, 1968; Oil on paper marouflaged onto canvas with gesso and gelatin, 72 × 54″

Published by Harry N. Abrams, Inc., New York
Gebr. Mann Verlag GmbH, Berlin
All rights reserved
No part of the contents of this book may be reproduced
without the written permission of the publishers
Library of Congress Catalogue Card No. 69–18329
Color transparencies by Ivor Protheroe
Photos of the artist by Helen Miljakovich
Printed in West Germany by Brüder Hartmann, Berlin

One never has all the facts,
yet a commitment must be made.

June Wayne

ACKNOWLEDGEMENTS

In the research and writing of this book I am primarily indebted to the artist who welcomed me to her studio in Los Angeles during the summer of 1968; recorded hours of tapes about her work at my request; and checked the text for correctness of detail. Throughout I have enjoyed working directly with the artist and greatly appreciated her keenness, wit, and candor.

Philip Rhys Adams, Director of the Cincinnati Art Museum, was instructive in our discussions about the book. Members of his staff whom I also thank for their valuable assistance include: Mrs. Alice P. Hook, Librarian; Miss Helen Pernice, Curatorial Secretary, Print Department; Mrs. Jane Larsen and Theodore Gantz.

In addition to my Museum colleagues, I wish to thank Miss Donna Tryon of Los Angeles for writing the documentation of Miss Wayne's graphics which was incorporated into the text and catalogue, and Mrs. Auriel Douglas of Los Angeles for her help in editing the text and biography. The following people contributed their unique talents and viewpoints: Dr. Abraham Kaplan, University of Hawaii; Peter Pollack, New York; Douglass Howell, Westbury, Long Island; Miss Jo Miller, Brooklyn Museum; and Ralph Ewers, Natural History Museum, Cincinnati. I appreciate their help and that of the collectors of Miss Wayne's work who corresponded with me concerning various details.

Thanks to my husband Denny who helped me in many ways, it was a pleasure to write this book.

MARY W. BASKETT, *Curator of Prints*
Cincinnati Art Museum

CONTENTS

LIST OF ILLUSTRATIONS

June Wayne, November, 1968

An Introduction to the Artist

"Alles ist immer noch ganz anders." CHRISTOPH ECKE
"Concordia discors" HORACE
"Discordia concors" DR. JOHNSON

9

June Wayne and her art have been caught up, over the period of the last thirty years, in the tensions, and in some cases the surprising compatibility, of real and seeming opposites; cerebration and emotion, innocence and guilt, the ascetic and the sensual, the organic and the geometric, the sacred and the profane. Her work particularly has been animated by, and is, in fact, the evidence of her struggles with the demon in each of these literal, verbal opposites; the demon which in the resolution of living and artistic problems shows itself unexpectedly unbound by the inevitability of merely verbal contradictions.

Miss Wayne conceives of her symbolic shapes, techniques, compositions and entire themes as moving through the intervening climate between such polar concepts, sometimes containing within themselves teasing contradictions, and sometimes, just as surely, revealing the integrity of fractious ideas.

Her life bears out the ambivalence of her philosophy. She is amused that as founder and director of the Tamarind Lithography Workshop in Los Angeles, she is thought to be both "trafficker in gold" and the "strange artist." However, precisely because hers is an intellectual vantage which itself moves and changes as uninhibitedly as the meanings of her symbols, as soon as she or her thought has been labeled, it has been mislabeled. As soon as one thinks he has reached the bottom, his head breaks the surface again. She recently wrote about her work a statement which would have been equally relevant twenty years ago, and at any interim in her career as an artist since then,

"My art tends to build by infiltration, winning people slowly and one at a time to my way of thinking. They learn to read my structures and symbols which are constructed of multilevels and take time to see."[1]

It is in her art, however, that the public has been exposed to her tantalizing philosophy. The humble mushroom, embossed on her lithographs, penned on her drawings, is one of her favorite and most ubiquitous symbols, conveying an admixture of both delight and death. Its slender stem and fleshy, pneumatic umbrella promise a female and gastronomic attractiveness. At the same time, it is ugly, saprophytic and poisonous and it has most recently become metaphorically representative of the atom bomb. The richness of these antithetical references makes the mushroom peculiarly appealing to her. It is quick to grow, quick to decay. To June Wayne, the mushroom has become the present. Hence a whole race of "mushroom people" with mushroom cap heads inhabit her work. Noting in 1956 that her colleague Rico Lebrun was painting the themes of meat stalls, the Crucifixion, and Buchenwald for which his style and method had been ready long before, she wrote,

"And I suppose I too am attracted by those things that are comfortable to my range. The trap of one's own cliches!"[2]

The mushroom, and her use of it as private and public symbol, is a single example of many which have served her as concrete illustrations of her philosophy. More importantly, they have served as tools in the dramatic solution to the intellectual and artistic problems posed by that philosophy.

This is not to suggest that June Wayne is unique in her recognition of Hegelian paradox or even in her devotion to its graphic representation. Nevertheless, her work and life afford a remarkable and consistent catalogue of one individual's conscious struggle with it. In support of this effort, she has ranged over and through a series of concepts and themes in a variety of media: Optics, Symbols, Narrative, Modules, Justice, Fables, John Donne and Lemmings. The mixture of these structures and contents in her work rarely limits it to a single level; other levels are present obviously or by implication. Nevertheless, Miss Wayne has focused on certain themes in distinct periods while permitting the others to fade or begin to grow in the penumbra of specific works. Therefore, dating them is only intended to pinpoint the period when a particular theme dominated her work. When single works, not related to a developed theme, are discussed and/or illustrated they are placed chronologically into a given period.

Aspects of Optics 1947-1952

The science of optics and its relation to art have, at different periods of history, fascinated artists. In the 1960's this fascination reached a culmination in the distinct and spirited school of Optical Art. Certain aspects of this concern with optics occur in June Wayne's work of the 1940's and have recurred, with shifting emphases, to this day. Among the aspects she has explored are the aberrations of linear perspective; the relation of central vision and focal points to peripheral vision; and eyepaths across the flat picture plane or into three dimensional space. Her artistic synthesis of these interests took shape as the result of a brief moment experienced while driving at a high speed through the Second Street Tunnel in Los Angeles in 1947. The breakup of forms rushing by the open car window contrasted vividly with the stationary focal point at the tunnel's end. She thereby postulated the idea that the physiology of focal versus peripheral vision probably contained clues to a new method for presenting the illusion of movement. Once this possibility occured to her, she posed increasingly complex optical experiments in her art. The events preceding that 1947 tunnel experience, reveal the background from which her interest sprang.

When Miss Wayne took a course in Production Illustration at the California Institute of Technology during World War II, she proved adept at translating aircraft blueprints into three dimensional drawings based on classic perspective. She inquired not only into the application of the rules of perspective but also into their breakdown. The so-called laws of perspective were seemingly not laws at all, but generalizations which hold only within limited angles of vision. She rationalized that at the point where the rules no longer apply, an opportunity for invention must exist for the artist.

After the war, she talked at length about these interests with art critic Jules Langsner. Their discussions concerning light theories, the science of optics and the art of impressionism were a prelude to the observation she made while driving through the tunnel. Two oil paintings, two lithographs, and a space construction all entitled "Tunnel," and executed between 1947–1951, resulted from these discussions, from her independent curiosity, and the culmination of these influences in her "experience." About a dozen additional works with other titles, variations on optical themes, exist in these three different media.

One or two of the eight constructions in space which were exhibited at the Santa Barbara Museum of Art in March of 1950, may be extant but their whereabouts is unknown. However, this type of experiment, incorporating a spatial dimension into one's graphic compositions, is familiar today. Robert Rauschenberg did this in his well publicized lithographic object, *Shades*, of 1964 and motorized silk-screen composition, *Revolvers*, of 1967. Marcel Duchamps' studies in optical constructions in the 1920's are an antecedent[3] although his pioneer works were not known to Wayne at the time of her experiments. On glass measuring about $12 \times 16''$, she mounted parts of colored ink drawings, some of which were figurative, some abstract.

The Cavern #2, January, 1951; lithograph, 21¹/₄ × 29¹/₈"

The layers of glass were placed in slotted frames. Focal areas were literally cut out of the drawings. As a result, when a spectator moved around a Wayne construction, he was witness to changing forms, with changing interrelationships. Looking back on this experience, the artist notes that she left these spatial experiments because the potential of the idea was so rich that she could have taken years or even a lifetime to exploit it fully, probably to the exclusion of experiments with other media which were more important to her.[4] Consequently, these space constructions were put aside and later she destroyed those she owned. However, the other medium, lithography, utilized by the artist to resolve optical problems, has become the mainstay of her creative reputation.

In the spring of 1948, while working on one of the space constructions, Miss Wayne could not resolve the problem of controlling one's eye movements from the periphery of the layered image to actual space. It occurred to her that a new medium might be more satisfactory as a vehicle to solution. The medium she chose was lithography. Here in black and white she was able to dispense with the complication of color. Her first lithographs show a rapid grasp of technique in their application of liquid tusche with brush and pen, drawing with lithographic crayon, and scratching lines with a sharp tool or with sandpaper. The printer with whom she collaborated in these and all subsequent editions through 1956, was Lynton R. Kistler whose embossed chop, a slanted "K" in a circle within a rectangle, appears with the Wayne mushroom on the prints. Cross-fertilization between media was natural to the artist and she worked in this manner from 1948–1954. Hence oil paintings from these years may have lithographic siblings and vice versa. Noting the advantages of working between media to bring new and different values to an artist's expression, Miss Wayne sports that "Pigeon holes are for pigeons."[5]

The painting *The Cavern* (color plate) represents a key moment in the artist's exploration of optics.[6] This painting's relation to a subsequently simplified lithographic version, *The Cavern #2* (illus.) is instructive. In each work both the perception of movement, which is a function of peripheral vision, and the perception of details, which is a function of central vision, are brought within the picture plane. A wide area of vision is, therefore,

Cavern, 1948; Oil on canvas, 35 × 54"

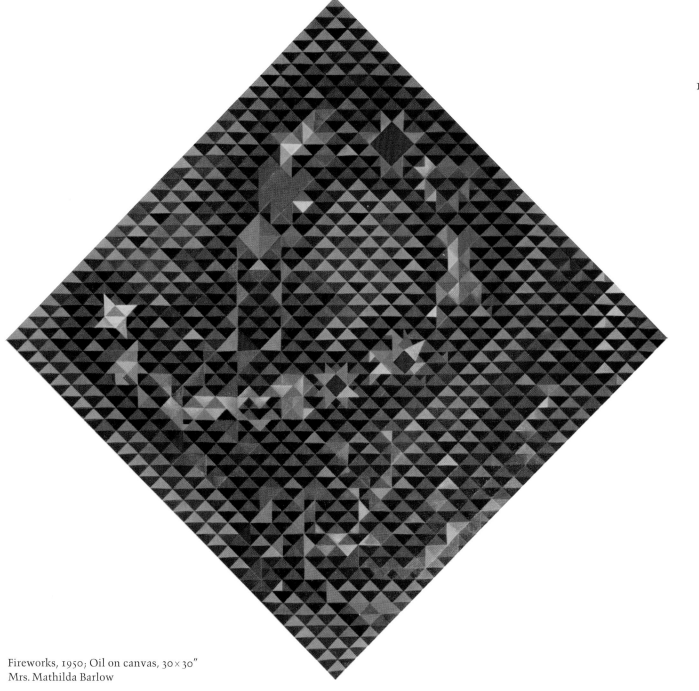

Fireworks, 1950; Oil on canvas, 30 × 30″
Mrs. Mathilda Barlow

Strange Moon, February, 1951; lithograph, $13^7/_8 \times 18^1/_8''$

compacted for the viewer in what the artist once called a "reverse cinerama." Furthermore, the third dimension of depth, a function of binocular vision, is built into the picture plane. With one eye closed and the other fixed in the black focal area to the left of center, one finds a definite heightening of the experience of shapes sailing from the background to the margin of the picture plane and into actual space.

The structure and discipline of the symbolic shapes themselves have been tightened in the lithograph to produce an image of startling strength. In the black focal area, the white paper is revealed to shape five objects: a mushroom, a bird-like creature, an egg, a hieroglyph-figure seated in profile, and a quite scientifically drawn nerve cell. Recognition of these ambiguous and/or specific shapes is, however, secondary to the shape apart from its meaning as it is propelled into the periphery by centrifugal force, and in this movement, transformed into primordial fantasy by combining with other shapes, such as the mushroom-bird-hand combination in the lower right corner.

Both painting and print delight in setting an emotional climate with the calculated use of symbolic shapes. The vibrant yellow and modulated purple-blue ambiance of the painting becomes, in the lithograph, a granular gray ground executed by spraying tusche onto the stone with a "Flit gun." The lithograph dramatizes in a black and white atmosphere the shift from white shapes on a black ground to black shapes on gray. Particularly in the print, peripheral shapes such as the devil and crystal head in the lower left corner predict later developments in the artist's work.

The diamond-shaped canvas, familiar to students of Piet Mondrian's modular work earlier in this century, gave Miss Wayne a novel format in which to explore her optical problems. Her 30 × 30" *Fire-works* painting of 1950 (color plate) facets the surface of a diamond into nine hundred small diamonds, thirty squares to a side. The triangles, which are one-half of these squares bisected diagonally, become the modules or standard units which are the basis of the entire design. Against a hot violet parquetry, the eyepath, disguised as a skyrocket, ascends, doubles back on itself, and explodes into the space at the right, coming to rest on two cool green flags. The three red and one brown square which plot the eyepath with focal points are transformed into hexagonal and octagonal voids as the rocket disintegrates.

A more complicated problem in eyepaths is solved in the lithograph, *Strange Moon* of 1951 (illus.); a painting of the same subject matter exists. Here the eyepath follows a moving moon or egg-shaped disk. This solid must not only cross over itself fluidly but travel in continuous motion through a texture. *Strange Moon*, which has been hung in all four directions, is a satisfying composition for many a contemporary viewer, accustomed as he is now to the floating disks of Larry Poons, the undulating stripes of Bridget Riley and the stretched checkerboards of Victor Vasarely.[7] To counter the geometry of this lithograph, which the artist felt was "too barren," the surface of the moving disk was embossed to give it the sensuous, organic surface of an egg shell. This was achieved by actually carving into the lithographic stone, like intaglio getting into lithography.[8]

The Target (illus.) and *The Tunnel # 2* (illus.), lithographs of February and July 1951 respectively,

The Tunnel #2, July, 1951; lithograph, 15¹/₂×19⁵/₈″

The Target, February, 1951; lithograph, 14$^1/_{16}$ × 17$^7/_8$"

reiterate with authority themes stated in earlier optical paintings, lithographs and space constructions. The former, like the painting, *The Lawcourt,* 1951, is composed of overlapping ovals that echo the bony rim of forehead and cheek through which we see. The target itself, a black spiral in a square white focal area, is placed in a visionary world, leaning back into a solid black void and surrounded by symbolic textures. Stone blocks project outward at the right; cobblestones, from the floor; a night sky with stars, to the left; and a pattern of elongated wing-like diamonds, from the ceiling. Again, as in *Strange Moon,* the geometric pairs with the organic. The calculated image, menacing in its formal perfection, is countered by the artist's use of pointed tools to stipple at random through liquid tusche and to cause a physical raising of the white area which twists into the black target. Similarly, her use of natural textures in the lights of *The Tunnel # 2,* is more successfully and completely developed in later work. Furthermore, both the black and grays of this lithograph were printed to the edge of the stone to encompass the inherent irregularity of the natural edges.

The weird trip through *The Tunnel # 2* is focused into deep space combined with the outward whirling movement of the tunnel walls. The latter become physically curved by the distortions of peripheral vision. The vanishing point down the cone of the tunnel is placed to the left of center, a printed reversal from *The Tunnel* painting. Both positions prove natural for a convincing vanishing point into the background and a centrifugal spiraling of the textured tunnel into the foreground. Donald Bear, former Director of the Santa Barbara Museum of Art, who gave Miss Wayne her first one-man show on the West Coast in 1950, was sensitive to the particular way in which, as he put it,

"In a sense she commands the spectator within the compass of her picture-space and the activity of the painting takes place around him. This is a problem which has received a completely different solution, and a more emotional one, by John Marin, the American watercolorist. June Wayne has used a different set of values, more rigid, mathematical, and for the most part, rather quietly ordered."[9]

True to the contradictions of the artist's thinking, the optical works, many of which no longer exist, actually continue to have a profound influence on her. Recently Wayne clarified the import of this period.

"In itself the physiology of vision is not a sufficient goal for me... I am interested in the relation between focal and peripheral vision because I am interested in the problem of movement... Since peripheral vision is the way in which we perceive movement and movement is the equivalent of time, as Einstein so cleverly pointed out, optics provided me another structural method for doing what I wanted to do."[10]

Symbol and Narrative 1949-1956

The Chase, February 28, 1949; Oil on canvas, 20×80″

At the same time that the artist worked on optics, she developed narratives using original, personal and fluid symbols. An understanding of eyepaths, of focal points, and of the breakdown of shapes in the periphery of vision, were all parts of a necessary technical vocabulary for the development of these narratives. The structural methods of optics gave her the tools to move symbols in the proper directions and sequences, at the proper speeds, to evoke the response she sought. Czech novelist Franz Kafka provided the climate for the symbols themselves. Highly personal "Wayne symbols" are therefore often referred to as "Kafka symbols." At sixteen, the artist, who at that time called herself by her first and middle name, June Claire, was introduced to Kafka's work by Harold Jacobson, a friend from the University of Chicago. Later, all during the war years, she carried a copy of Kafka's *The Castle* with her to the many places she lived.

"Kafka created parallels for the world I was experiencing. And his deceptively simple style intensified the anxieties he described."[11]

These same ambiguous frustrations and tensions were what she brought to her world of lines, textures, and colors when, in her thirties, she was occupied with symbols and narratives. With contempt for obvious associations, the artist points out that her symbols are not specific but resonant in their environments. Therefore, any literal reading of the sixteen symbols of *Kafka Symbols, Second Version*, 1949 (illus.) is not only superficial but misleading. The fact that these six-

Kafka Symbols, Second Version, February, 1949
lithograph, 27³/₄ × 21³/₄″

The Elements, 1951; Oil in wax on canvas, 27 × 90″

teen figures do, however, compose a vocabulary for many works of this period makes the artist's own comments about them helpful, at least in pointing out the atmosphere within which an individual symbol has meaning to her. From top to bottom, left to right are references to: the trumpet in Kafka's *Amerika*; an eye, sperm and egg on a table; a knave with crowned head and a "Club" foot; a sadistic figure; a primordial figure; a toy-like figure with dominant phallus adapted from a chiasma of optic nerves; Kafka's *Castle* and flag on a foot; a mushroom with soft halo cap and saw-toothed root; a variation of the primordial figure; the mole in Kafka's *Burrow*; a cross section of a nerve bundle echoing the club foot; an abstrac-

tion; a seated birdfrog; a triple mushroom-headed hourglass; an elaborate statement of a five-fingered hand with two fingers raised making the Kohen sign of the Jewish high priests; and a castle-church.[12] These symbols are treated like heraldry in their placement against four distinct vertical environments. Their overall impact is less dependent on either Kafka or Miss Wayne than on the viewer's own lambent imagination.

The knave and triple mushroom hourglass from *Kafka Symbols, Second Version* become the protagonists in the oil painting, *The Chase*, 1949 (color plate). The competitors race from left to right a distance of eighty inches. In doing so, they traverse their individual stripes of color, flat bands of gray and orange each scaled in a proportion of one to eight, and reminiscent of the scale of an Asian format for narrative, the hand scroll. At times the speed, or perhaps excitement, of either or both of the figures spins it in and out of the sharp focus which is the temper of this meticulously executed canvas.

The artist commented extensively on the content and technique of this painting in the catalogue for the exhibition, *Contemporary American Painting* in Chicago in 1951. In this comment, she revealed quite a remarkable affection for her symbols and empathy with the story in which they were involved.

"The Chase is one of a series of works expressing an attitude on the predicament of man. It uses two characters out of a vocabulary of symbols on which I have been working for a long time. As you see, it is a painting with a 'moral,' for the victor, by the time he has completed his race across the canvas, has assumed the characteristics of the loser, and vice versa. Nevertheless, the prevailing spirit of the painting is humorous and indulgent.

About method: *The Chase* reflects my interest in the relation between optics and the aesthetic visual experience. I have developed what seems to be (for me) a useful method for controlling the eyepath of the observer. This method helps me to determine the sequence, rhythm and speed with which my paintings are 'read.' *The Chase* uses these optical controls to accomplish the sense of moving sequence without which the painting could not make its point.

In addition to communicating a rewarding pattern or configuration, I am trying to involve the spectator more deeply, and on other levels. We live in a confused age without a widespread heritage of meaningful symbols. Yet, sometimes the artist helps to crystallize and create symbols, as well as utilizing those already available. For me these may be found somewhat readily in the predicament of our times, and they are interpretable in new ways as a result of our increased knowledge of the human psyche. At any rate, through these channels, allegory once again seems a real possibility to me."[13]

Kafka is not mentioned as a source of the symbolic climate since this painting, to be appreciated, like all her developed works, stands independent of the need for literary associations. However, once knowing the source and content of those associations, a chain of reactions on that level (her private level as it were) become part of the viewer's response. For example, Wayne has been intrigued by Kafka's thought which seems often to move in and out of focus within the structure of a single sentence, changing subject and direction to confound the ambiguities of a given situation. The symbols in *The Chase* essentially follow that pattern.

In contrast to the lively social satire of *The Chase*, a similarly structured horizontal narrative painting, *The Elements* (color plate) of two years later, makes a harmonic counterpoint of the primary

The Hero, December, 1949; lithograph, $27^{1}/_{2} \times 2I^{3}/_{4}''$

substances of the universe. The composition of the latter painting is complicated one step beyond that of the former. Not only do the figures transmute as they move through their own distinct environments, but two of the elements literally cross over the third to exchange their environments.

In a slightly more elongated format with a proportion of one to ten, versus the one to eight module of *The Chase,* the horizontal bands of blue-gray, black and gray-brown are the environments respectively for earth as seen in a scientifically correct cluster of sand crystals, a construct for fire and one for water. The faceted cluster transmutes to spirit as figured in a fancifully winged object; water, to life as figured in the anatomical heart; and fire, to death, being extinguished as it moves through two atomic rain-snow passages. The critical point of the composition is that place where the themes cross. As in *Strange Moon,* the smoothly rhythmic crossover of two orbits is accomplished through a delicate balance between the eyepath and the double-entendre of dual direction to that eyepath at this critically complex point.

Because it was essential to the viewer to be able to encompass the entire rhythmic sequence of *The Elements* in one glance, any reflections on the surface of the oil paint would have been distracting. Therefore this painting was a first experiment in the use of oil paint in a wax medium to achieve a pristine matte surface.

Neither of these two paintings in the narrative context of the artist's work has been attempted by her in lithography. To develop these narratives,

The Retreat, April, 1950; lithograph, $13^{15}/_{16} \times 20^{1}/_{8}''$

actual physical size and space were needed, and this uninterrupted horizontal space was not practical in print formats. To compensate by reducing the scale of the images would, the artist says, have made them finical. However, in one instance the artist presents an engaging, satirical, continuous narrative in both a large rectangular lithograph of $28 \times 21^{1}/_{2}''$ (illus.) and a $30 \times 40''$ painting entitled *The Hero,* 1949. The story line follows the fortunes and misfortunes of the toy-like hero who figures in her earlier Kafka vocabulary of symbols. The hero may be Kafka's Joseph K., Karl Rossmann, or Thomas Mann's Felix Krull, or may, more generally, represent a metaphor of all heroes who are themselves in spite of themselves. Through focal areas of detail, movement, emphasis and rest, the hero moves across the top of the picture, falls to a center level, picks himself up to travel from right to left, falls again, this time to the bottom of the picture plane, where he bounces up a rocky projection, and ends hanging by his own flag.

One single moment is captured in *The Retreat, 1950* (illus.) another lithograph which develops a figure from the vocabulary of "Kafka Symbols." In its broadest sense the print satirizes all people who retreat into their shells. Specifically, this creature with a mole mask behind his neck and the Bodhisattva's jeweled "urna" in his forehead, carries the tone of the narrator in Kafka's short story, *The Burrow.* The textures within the dark womb are executed with brush, pen and crayon; the surrounding atmosphere, with sprayed tusche. Although this print is technically expert, its popularity is, of course, as is usual, based on the image. The artist has found this popularity as quizzical as the image. By referring to the female muscle sheath in the oval at the right of the black uterus and to a subterranean creature at the left of it, the overtone was intended to be physiological and hence repulsive.[14]

The same type of engaging but enigmatic figure as *The Hero* and the burrower in *The Retreat* is "The Quiet One." Particularly in the painting (color plate), the excessively thin, erect organism in the vertical coffin-shaped niche attracts one's sympathy while it bides its time, "legs crossed,"

The Quiet One, June 20, 1949; Oil on canvas, 30 × 14"
Dr. and Mrs. Leonard Rosengarten

27

trying to conceal a crystal in its "hands." Six months after this painting was completed, another version, which Miss Wayne first developed in drawings, was pulled from a stone. This lithograph (illus.) changed the organism's environment from a protected quiet to a threatening quiet.[15] The diametric shift within the emotion was achieved by literally closing off the corridor with a black plane immediately behind the creature and surrounding it with crayon textures or sharp penned textures, the outer limits of which are modular triangles within a black frame. The painting is especially benign in contrast, admitting as it does, light from behind the figure and surrounding it with a series of flat tranquil colors from light gray and blue in the periphery to the cool blues and greens closer to the figure. This is a prime example of the artist's interest and skill in changing the emotional climate of a symbol.

"The Witnesses," as subjects for paintings and lithographs dating from 1950, 1952 and 1956, have been classed as often with the Justice series as with the Kafka Symbols or Narrative series. As pointed out in the introduction, Miss Wayne rarely limits her work to single themes but moves freely among themes. She thoroughly enjoys, as she puts it, "being discursive in my art."

Each of *The Witnesses* (illus.) is trapped in his own environment, as are the coffin-bound "quiet ones" previously discussed, and the jurors who figure in

Quiet One, January, 1950; lithograph, 20⅝ × 11¹⁵/₁₆″

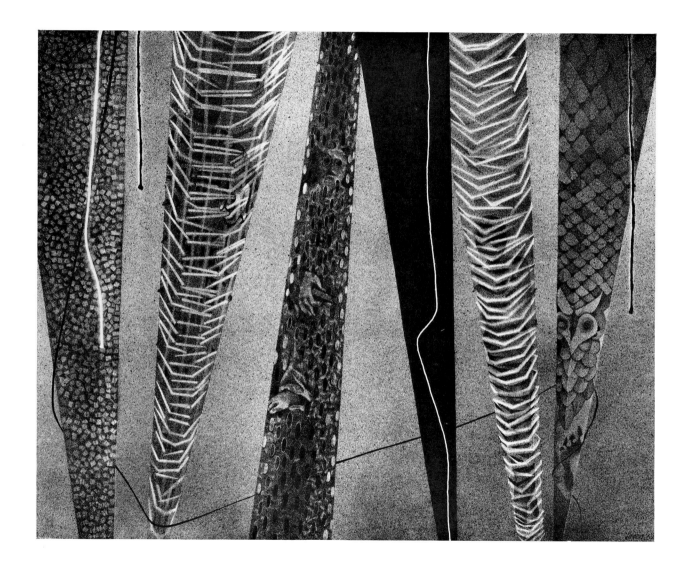

The Witnesses II, First Version, September, 1952; lithograph, $22^7/8 \times 28^3/4''$

the Justice series. She has thereby suggested that man sees and comprehends through and within his own limits; in the case of each witness, through and within tubular vision. Therefore man is his own prisoner. Sinister, too, is the fact that the witnesses are not clearly delineated but are evoked as a secondary vision from textured tubes, the primary foci. With skill and imagination the artist explored the movements within these textures and how they were affected by scale, by color and by compositional variants. The illustrated lithograph tests the effectiveness of string as a compositional device to wind both tautly and limply through the conical tubes. Inked and uninked strings were actually placed on the stone to emboss the print surface. Small square objects, slivers of wood and poppy seeds were used here as in other "The Witnesses" lithographs as stop-outs over which liquid tusche was sprayed. The stop-outs were brushed from the stone after the tusche dried and were modified with crayon and pen overdrawing to give the resulting textures to the tubes.[16]

The artist has recently said that she would like to attack the subject of "The Witnesses" again – "much, much larger ... (and with) no color."[17] Something of the necessary menace of the image was removed by the use of the yellow-golds and carmines in the paintings. Furthermore, black and white are a passion with the artist who, like the Chinese artist-scholar, sees in black every color and every possibility for rich nuance. It has been through lithography that this passion has been exploited. Black and white have two additional fascinations for Miss Wayne. With them, the potential for positive-negative space is great. Furthermore, when working with the close values of one or the other opposite, the artist is challenged to "see how close he can come to the edge without falling off."[18]

In summation, the Kafka reference reinforces the artist's fundamental way of seeing things, that is, ambiguously poised between polarized concepts. Narratives were an opportunity to use aspects of optics long known to science but untouched by artists before Miss Wayne.

Crystalline Modules 1950-1958

Seeing a world of fantasy through transparent, crystalline modules became June Wayne's way of seeing during the fifties. Dividing a flat picture plane into modules, or standard units of measure, was the beginning of this development. The modules were usually squares, rectangles, triangles, diamonds or parallelograms used singly or in combination within a composition. In accordance with the idea of the module, proportional relationships consisting of repeats of the design within the design were established by means of these standard units. At the beginning they composed, in the artist's context, only a section of the image as in the lithograph, *Quiet One,* 1950 (illus.), or they composed every section without using any shapes outside themselves as in the painting, *Fireworks,* 1950 (color plate). In both these cases the more sophisticated and unique direction which was Miss Wayne's final statement of the crystalline module was yet to come. When it reached the end of its evolution her modules became transparent or crystalline and actually resembled crystals. Through certain transparent sections, fantastic icons were modeled.

The excitement behind the concept of the module has been articulated by California architect Ezra D. Ehrenkrantz in his article "Modular Materials and Design Flexibility."[19] Although Professor Ehrenkrantz made specific references to architecture, his ideas open and enliven the whole sphere of the module, particularly the painted, printed and drawn ones at hand.

According to Ehrenkrantz, a modular system is not a limiting construct of specific measurements but rather, an ordered conceptual framework within which creative ideas can be freely constructed, structured and disciplined. He points out that the validity of modular components is based on the fact that they relate to each other in a way similar to the way that notes of a keyboard relate to each other. The architect, contractor and mason must instinctively understand the module just as the composer, conductor and pianist must understand the keyboard. The order of both the keyboard and module is absolute although its ability to be varied is limitless. The module then indicates a disciplined freedom and an infinite potential resulting from a union of opposites.[20]

With an intuitive feeling for the module as keyboard and for its discipline and freedom in painting and graphics, June Wayne then picked up those directions of her earlier work which could be pushed further within this conceptual framework. In the first case, she again used aspects of optics to move the eye through the module in order to convey a sense of rhythm and to communicate energy. The artist is fond of drawing a parallel here to a move in the game of billiards where, in a line of three balls, the first ball is hit hard while it and the second ball are held. The end ball which is not held spins off; its energy is communicated through the middle ball. This is, by simile, the same transmission of energy and bounce which she conveys through her modules.

In the second case, the artist brings her interest in weighting the emotional significance of symbols to her modular works. Through the modular framework, there is an attempt to communicate an emotion sympathetic to the modeled image. In the case of the lithograph, *The Bride* (illus.), the module can be read as an oval which seductively echoes the shape of her navel and breasts.

A possible parallel can be drawn between the crystalline modules of June Wayne's work and the dream world of crystals evoked in the one novel by the late Herbert Read entitled *Green Child.* The artist read this book in the mid-fifties. Aldous Huxley's book, *Heaven and Hell,* published in 1956, which came to the artist's attention in that year, also provided literary confirmation of the artist's crystalline images. Huxley points out that visionaries experience Paradise replete with jewels, facets and crystals. Miss Wayne, commenting at a pragmatic level on Huxley's ecstatic report of these paradisiac visions, suggested that "jeweled, tesselated, mosaic patterns can be produced at will by permitting the water of one's shower to beat against the closed eyelids. The force of the water drops probably stimulates after-images of the rods and cones of the eye."[21]

The Sanctified, which was printed as a lithograph in 1950 (illus.) and painted in 1951 (color plate), does not totally integrate modeled figures with the crystalline modules, although it advances in that direction. The angels with feathered wings, at the top of the picture, stare through the triangular modules of the background. Actually they are disjointed parts of angels, not complete figures. The male and female toward the bottom of the picture signal to each other through the diamond modules of the rectangle which fades into the checkered floor. They are primarily hands, feet and faces, again not complete figures. However, the monk-executioner figure who stands in an isosceles triangle does not appear through either of these modules, but in front of them. He is anchored into the composition by means of the two light triangles immediately below his feet. Although an abstraction, he is fullbodied and unaffected by the dissolution into modules which is going on around him.

The emotional associations of the subject are both sacred and profane. The couple at the feet of the "sanctified one" could be in provocative pursuit of one another. The angels could be voyeurs. In the lithograph, the "sanctified one," who at first glance looks quite holy in his hood and robe, holds an obvious phallic symbol and may indeed be more the hangman than the monk. In both interpretations he shines by his own light, not having, therefore, to depend on power from outside himself for enlightenment. The painting which was conceived after the lithograph, turned a horizontal composition into a vertical one. This permitted the effective emphasis of the hooded figure in an elongated triangle of light, thus further sharpening the contradiction of his ambivalent reference.

Right after completing *The Sanctified* lithograph, the artist commented that she had particularly enjoyed doing its tesselated floor.[22] Her obvious pleas-

The Sanctified, December, 1950; lithograph, $13^3/4 \times 17^7/8''$

33

The Sanctified, 1951; Oil in wax
on canvas, 40×30"
Mr. and Mrs. Benjamin B. Smith

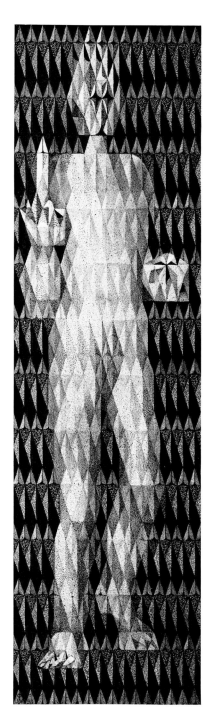

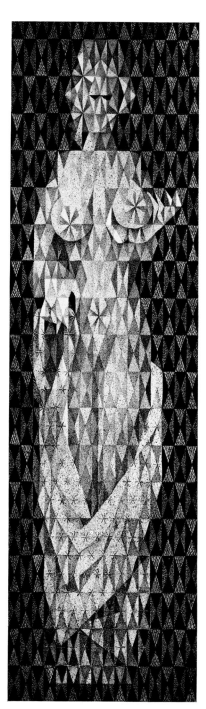

ure in modeling figures through crystalline modules received its most complete statement soon after this in the impressive triptych, *The Suitor, The Advocate* and *The Bride* (illus.) which has a frieze intended to be seen above it entitled *The Dreamers* (illus.). These four separate compositions exist as both paintings and lithographs. The fact that they were planned as a unit did, however, dictate a uniform size to the vertical and horizontal formats and in the case of the triptych, a uniform module in a three to one proportion.

The suitor's module stresses a black vertical, thereby weighting the masculinity of his climate. He carries what might be a candle or a phallic symbol in his right hand, a crystal in his left. The advocate's module is a diamond bisected vertically into black and gray halves, indicating neutrality. His dominant gesture points the index finger of his left hand into the palm of his right hand. The gesture supports the authority of his counsel. The bride's module, as noted before, heightens her femininity. She delicately holds up part of her gown between the thumb and index finger of her right hand, while the rest of the gown falls below her hips. Her left hand holds her breast, which resembles both her module and a crystal. The dreamers, a reference to the united bride and suitor, are seen in a sensual horizontal twist through a module

The Bride, December, 1951
The Advocate, January, 1952
The Suitor, December, 1951; lithographs, $27^1/_2 \times 7^7/_8$" each

which, in this case, the artist jokes, was weighted to "screen their privacy."

Each figure has a crystalline or diamond-shaped cap for a head which, when added to the faceted surface, makes the fact of their corporeal, fleshy memory in the viewer's mind, all the more remarkable. Each figure breaks out of his module in certain sections which are thereby emphasized. This deviation from the module usually occurs in the areas of the hands and the feet. The animation of each surface carries the eye of the viewer in and out of the modules to weave through the rhythms established by the artist. The eyepath through the modules of the dreamers is particularly active since the proportional relations of the small triangles to the larger triangles and to the even larger landscape of triangles are so expertly handled.

The paintings of the bride and suitor show them posed almost weightless on a pillow of their bed. The painted figures are smaller in relation to the compositions than in the lithographs; their symbols, more specific. The large painting of the advocate shows him standing on a sphere into which he drops a continuous string of moon-shaped coins which rise again into his hands. The large painting of *The Dreamers* (color plate & detail) does not vary the basic composition of the lithograph. However, the figures in the painting have more space around them to accommodate an even more vigorous moving back and forth of the picture plane through the proportional triangular modules. The pink and green triangles of the dreamers' bodies effectively translate into flesh tones.

The Dreamers, 1952; Oil on canvas, 21 × 63″
Dr. and Mrs. Lyman Harrison

The Dreamers, detail

Eve tentée, 1958
Adam en attente, 1958; lithographs, each 31¹/₂ × 9¹/₂″

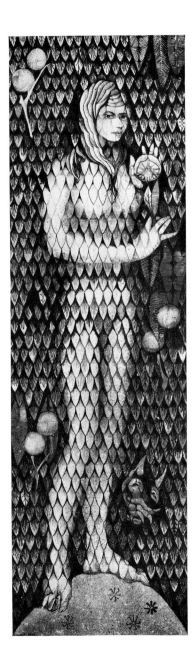

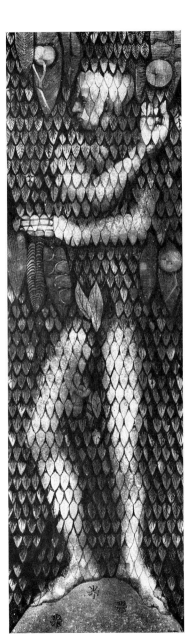

In some of the paintings and lithographs, but particularly in the drawings of this period, the modules are only developed in the area of the figures, leaving the background blank. These works demonstrate an ability to use empty space as an active participant in the composition. Both the drawings, "Study for the Bride" and "The Awakened" are fine examples of this ability.

In many ways the triptych explored here anticipates the *Adam en attente* (Adam waiting) – *Eve tentée* (Eve tempting) lithographic diptych of 1958 (illus.). Adam and Eve's crystalline module has been changed, however, from the precision of the earlier ruled module to the freedom of a biological module. Although these units are also reminiscent of a coat of mail, the reference to veined leaves is probably stronger and supports this more casual and subtle organic appearance, where neither the module itself, nor its pattern, is rigidly drawn.[23]

The two figures stand with their feet firmly planted on the top or perhaps on the bottom of the world. Instead of tempting Adam with an apple, Eve holds up a mushroom, the artist's favored symbol of delight and death. In fact, the mushroom is drawn, in this case, to resemble the surrounding apples. It is also similar in shape to the breast-crystal of *The Bride* (illus.). The horned head of Satan appears near Eve's feet. Adam's head seems to be illuminated from within, a characteristic of the mushroom cap worn by the mushroom people which are illustrated later. He is obviously brooding while waiting in a very stylized, yet convincing, posture of classical sculpture.

The success of these images has been phenomenal. They have been pirated for reproductions from Los Angeles to the Bahamas. The three original editions were printed on white wove, grey laid and beige wove paper respectively (see Catalogue: Lithographs, nos. 108 and 109). Eve's apples in some of the impressions in each of these editions have been hand-tinted in rose by the artist.

Adam and Eve would lend themselves to a tapestry interpretation, an idea which the artist still hopes to use. Earlier, she had attempted to translate other modular works into mosaics with the assistance of a California tile factory. That became a frustrating, unproductive experience because of the conflict between the slow monotony of the stone work and the fast tempo of Miss Wayne's creativity. In all developed works within the crystalline module series, the dichotomy, basic to the artist's intention, is that of the corporeal versus the ethereal. Fleshy, substantive figures are called out of the ethereal climate of transparent, crystalline modules. These works of art are able, therefore, to fuse visually a seemingly incompatible verbal contradiction.

The Messenger from the Jury 1953-1955

By September of 1953, the artist was beginning to address herself to the issues of the jury and in a larger context, to Justice. Not only had she wanted for many years to capture the emotional climate of Franz Kafka's *The Trial* but at this particular time she witnessed an actual trial.[24] The anxieties of the accused and of the accusers provided invaluable insight. The details of the case were, however, of less concern to the artist than the fundamental issues of guilt and innocence, and their contradictions. For example, in the earlier lithograph, *The Witnesses* (illus.), an underlying assumption had been that only the innocent would be free from anxiety if they suspected that they were being observed. In fact the mere suspicion that they were being observed might already be a sign of guilt.

The major work defining the Justice series is *The Messenger* painting of 1955 (color plate). It was the artist's largest canvas to that date, 60×50". This painting was the culmination of two years of study during which she completed about forty works which developed its component parts: the jury, the defendants and the messenger from the jury to the defendants. The jury was the first of these parts to be studied. In a lithograph by that title (illus.) of September 1953, six coffin-like jury boxes house or actually imprison, like the tubes of *The Witnesses*, five jurors. The artist insinuates that one juror is always absent or at least absent-minded! The jurors belong to the "Waynian" race of mushroom people. They are typically thin, vulnerable, asexual nudes who have illuminated mushroom caps for heads and who, in this case, examine the globes of light which they hold. The composition weaves in and out of positive-negative planes in shallow space through which the figures are seen. In this print, the artist, for the first time, scattered sand particles onto the stone as stop-outs spraying thin mists of liquid tusche over them. This technique resulted in a fine organic texture of black and white dots in a granular foil to the bright lights and flat black shadows. Both the method and the resulting texture are fundamental to her technical vocabulary.

In the lithograph *Final Jury* (illus.) printed four months later, in January of 1954, the jury box is simplified at the same time that it is made less specific so that it pulls in more spectrums of interpretation. This jury box, which is carried over quite literally into *The Messenger* painting, has overtones of church pews, high back chairs, triangular modules, pyramids, folded paper, crystals. It develops out of a series of drawings and a lithograph, *Second Jury,* of December, 1953. Without the globular lights to examine, these twelve jurors, some bored to somnolence, some as taut as their modules, face, and appear to judge, the viewer. This creates a tension in the lithograph which is different from that of the painting where the defendants are the object of the juror's attention and/or evil lack of attention.

The lithograph of *The Travellers* (illus.) composed of the two figures who become the defendants in *The Messenger* painting, is one of the most ambiguous and evocative images in the artist's œuvre.

A Work of Mourning III
February, 1953; Donald Bear Series; lithograph,
$31^3/4 \times 24''$

The Messenger
1955; Oil on canvas, 60×50″

Third Study for the Messenger, November, 1954; Ink spray, pen and ink, 12³/₄×10″

This couple within a crystal are wrapped in the bed sheet of love and in the winding sheet of death. The lines which describe their crystal, their two bodies and their sheet, delight the artist who has here been able to point out that air is never more ethereal than when placed next to something solid. The polarization of opposites heightens both extremes.

In this lithograph the artist includes the semi-circular ridges at the edge of the stone in the composition to balance the control and cerebration of the image by emphasizing its opposite, in this case, the natural stone. The radiant atmosphere of the print was achieved with a stop-out of fine grains of salt and sand. Also in the painted version, the physical grains of sand are embedded in the paint to give natural texturing to the surface. The

The Jury, September, 1953; lithograph, 18×14³/₄″

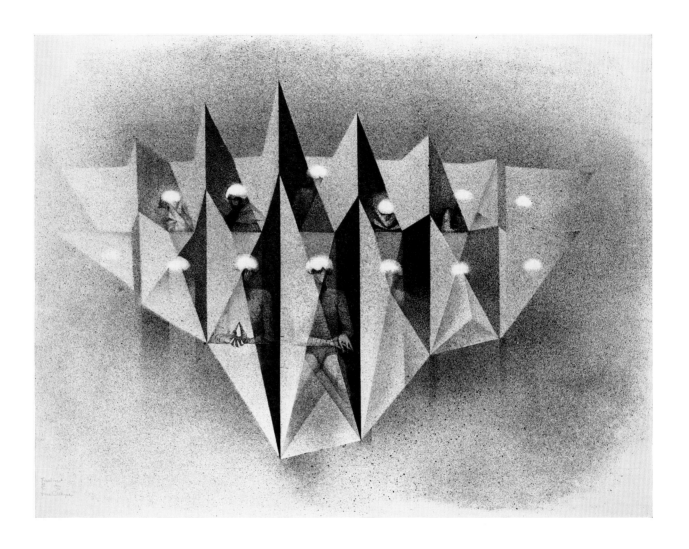

Final Jury, January, 1954; lithograph, 23¹/₄×32″

The Travellers, August, 1954; lithograph, $25^1/_4 \times 18^1/_2''$

Study for a Messenger V, January, 1955; lithograph, 18⁷/₈×26″

artist considers natural objects and textures to be essential to her work because they provide a bit of tangible reality, and thus lend credibility to the image. These objects and textures "mislead one into believing."[25]

The figure of the messenger, studied in drawings and in a lithograph of this period, disengages himself from the jury box, drifts down the right side of the painting, passes behind the defendants, and stops in mid-air to illuminate the defendants' crystal. The drawing reproduced here (illus.) shows him in the last phase of his travels. He is vertical with his face to the spectator, holding a light in his left hand. A horizontal position for the messenger was tested in the lithograph *Study for a Messenger V* (illus.) which also exists in a painted version. Five standing creatures witness the messenger's visitation which occurs from left to right in a side stroke through the air, parallel to the picture plane. The figure second from the left crosses his fingers for luck, evidently not trusting what this visitation may bring. It is the sparkling, illuminated climate, not the messenger's position, which then advances into the climactic painting, *The Messenger*. While still in the midst of working on this canvas in 1955, the artist, after describing its sequence of events, told of the suspense in bringing it to fulfillment, "It is a beautiful idea, with an evocative look about it . . . and even the study is very gripping. But it will be my most difficult work to accomplish . . ."[26]

The importance of this painting lies both in its summation of the artist's ideas on the subject of Justice, and in its summation of several currents in her stylistic development. It also presages future directions in that development. For *The Messenger*, Wayne freely and unselfconsciously used optical devices for narration, the twist of symbolic ambiguities, and the figure in a module. The ambiance of the forthcoming Fables and of the John Donne series is here first presented. It is a highly significant moment in the artist's development.

June Wayne's work rounded a major thematic direction as a result of her association with Dr. Abraham Kaplan in the "fable project." She coordinated images with his text which she conceived as illustrations for Kaplan's fables, but images foreshadowed by her earlier and contemporaneous explorations of the jury and messenger figures. In a sense, of course, many of her prior works, both paintings and lithographs, were fables, and either contained within themselves the seeds of narrative or exampled full-blown narrative concepts. The fable project was thus a natural extension of June Wayne's innate predilection for complex interrelations of plot and character in a single, or a series of connected works.

However, in one sense the project differed from the others and instilled a new element in the artist's work. In this project the Waynian images are more or less directly responsive to Kaplan's narrative. In her earlier efforts, the narrative element is almost entirely a Waynian construct tenuously founded on outside sources. For example, the Kafka works owe little to that writer. She shares a point of view but not specific content. The trend begun in the fable project does itself reach maturity in Wayne's Donne-inspired works, where the discipline imposed by her source material adds a fertile dimension to the personal vision with which she imbues it as it passes into her own interpretations. Unfortunately the project as a whole did not reach completion in the fifties. Kaplan and Wayne had hoped to publish their book as a "livre de luxe" during that time but except for the production of six lithographs, the book is in limbo. Both artist and writer were interrupted by other commitments. Nevertheless, to the extent realized, the project is a delightful revelation of a collaborative effort to update, in a new format, historical, religious and fairyland fables beginning with God's creation of man.

The lithograph, *The First Critic* of July, 1955 (illus.) illustrates the climactic moment of the Kaplan fable by that title. The text reports that God transformed the angel, Lucifer, into the devil, Satan, for impertinently questioning the skill, and by implication the wisdom of God's creation, the first man.

"What Satan had asked was, 'What's it supposed to be?' MORAL: The hell of it is, sometimes the critics are right."[28]

The neutral gray atmosphere of silvery brilliance in which the defrocking occurs originated in, and evolved from, the Justice series. God is, metaphorically, the nebulae in the upper right corner, flooding light across the awkward young man on the left. For Wayne, the creation of a "new embodiment of the Devil" posed the real challenge. She wrote to Kaplan about her problem of the "new Devil" and received in reply this philosophical solution if not the artistic one:

"Your problem, a new embodiment of the Devil, is a hopeless one. He is the Devil precisely because there is no newness in him; behind the

The First Critic, July, 1955; lithograph, $26^7/8 \times 19''$

49

Tower of Babel A, August, 1955; lithograph,
$26^7/8 \times 19^1/4''$

The Saint and the Sinner, April, 1956; Oil on canvas, 20×60"

cliché of his appearance there is nothing but Emptiness (which is why he is so easily confused with God)."[29]

Finally, after numerous drawings of traditional horned devils, the unique image in the lithograph was put together. Wayne, obviously pleased by her solution, wrote to Kaplan:

"I believe I have the devil by the tail. I believe I have solved the imagery. The devil is seen floating on his side, head resting superciliously on his arm. His right wing is radiant and floats up-

ward. His left wing is simply a series of abstract slashes of black reminiscent of lightning formation but more formal. Down his back runs a pattern of flames, two of which anticipate a tail later on. His head is a trident-like shape, largely irradiated with light from the 'god' area."[30]

The *Tower of Babel A* (illus.) relates to the Kaplan fable, "The Root Misunderstanding." According to this fable, the builders of the Tower of Babel, the High Priest and subsequent groups of people who climbed to heaven via the Tower of Babel, there found only a profound nothingness. But when they returned to earth they gave conflicting interpretations of what they thought they had seen.

"As for the 'confusion of tongues,' this refers to nothing other than the muddle of travellers' tales. MORAL: Even if you've been there, keep your ideas of Heaven to yourself."

The lithograph illustrated, one of three for this fable, is a detail of the arrival in Heaven at the top of the rocky tower. Seven isolated figures confront the silent void. The three who compose a triangle on the rocks in the foreground wear individual textures to stress almost a difference of "race" or tribe separating them. One resembles a circus acrobat with ropes tied around its furry body; one is encased in a black webbing; and the other's body is a crystalline patchwork, his head, a mushroom cap. Another mushroom person has stopped for a moment in his climb up the steep pillars of rocks to the left. The underlying simplicity and discipline of this composition in linear flow parallels the elegance of Chinese calligraphy. *Tower of Babel B*, another detail of the rocks of the tower, shows a different group of figures during their ascent. *Tower of Babel C* is the over-all view of mass movements of figures spiraling up and down the tower.

Each lithograph for the Fable series was printed on the German-made Miehle press, a high-speed, offset press used primarily for commercial lithography. Since Lynton Kistler had discontinued hand-printing from stones by this time, it was nec-essary for Wayne to accommodate herself to his commercial press. The sensitive fine grained backgrounds, the textures in the atmosphere and in the figures, were the result of Miss Wayne's preparation of the zinc plates with small particles of natural materials for stop-outs; specifically, sand, chips of glass, peas, beans, bits of wood, twigs and small pebbles. She then sprayed the plates with mists of tusche from an airbrush. The imaginative preparation and the cloud of spray combined to advantage with the quick touch of the high speed press, resulting in the sumptuous, yet fragile, silver-gray lustre of each of these lithographs.

One painting, *The Saint and the Sinner* of April 1956 (color plate) was also based on a Kaplan fable by that title. The story tells of a sinner frightened by word in the city that the Messiah is coming. As he flees on his donkey, he is met by a saint to whom he confesses his sins and resulting anxieties.

"When the godly one pointed out to him that a life of peripatetic anxiety was itself the bitter fruit of wickedness, the sinner was momentarily brought up short. But when he replied that he could not repose confidence in a Redeemer who could be outrun by a donkey, it was the saint who was plunged into thought. That night the holy man stole the sinner's ass and himself made his escape. MORAL: If your sins don't find you out, someone else's will."

Wayne's painting deliberately refers to Sienese narrative paintings of the fourteenth century. On reading this Kaplan fable, she was impressed that it had a "medieval town quality" in its opening paragraphs and she wagered that the town was probably Siena. The continuous narrative in a long horizontal format, in which the same figure in different attitudes relating to the story appears in consecutive areas of the painting left to right, was a device of medieval Sienese painting; it was also, of course, as we have seen in *The Chase* of 1949 and *The Elements* of 1951, a device used by her prior to this time. The new and specific reference to the Sienese lies in the painting's color, a studied recapture of the strident Sienese reds and blues. It was not executed, however, by painting in tempera color over gesso plaster and verdaccio shadows as in the case of Sienese painting, but instead by using oil underpainting in green and ochre and then similarly enriching the color through multiple glazes. The rock on which the abandoned sinner stands in the lower right corner is calculated to be reminiscent of landscape formation in medieval Italian painting.

The almost incredible speed of the sinner in flight from his sins; the subsequently combined shapes of both his and the saint's figures with the ass in single, separate abstract patterns; and the undulating eyepath left to right, recall Wayne's earlier narrative paintings and lithographs. Certainly this is a prime example of the artist using her virtuoso ability to present a narrative monitored as if by an optical metronome.

Love Poetry by John Donne 1956-1959

The prints and drawings which record June Wayne's reaction to John Donne's love poems are among the most acclaimed in her œuvre.[31] They were "mined out of long, cool, intense nights" while listening to recordings by Christopher Hassall and others, declaiming, as was their poet's intention, the intellectual passion of his love poetry. This project was started in the fall of 1956, when she worked in her Londonderry Place studio.

Although some 350 years separated John Donne's thought from the artist's personal catalogue of its power, logically these two creativities could be superimposed. Donne, as chief spokesman for the metaphysical poets at the beginning of the 17th century, thought within a framework appealing to Miss Wayne. Both artist and poet sought a cult similarity in polar dissimilarity and the integrity of fractious literal opposites. The twist of the intellectual and the sensual, for example, winds, like Ariadne's thread, through each. Yet never did the artist profess to be a Donne scholar; through her work she only meant to express his profound effect on her. Because she shares Donne's philosophical approach, she was successful in this endeavor on levels beneath and beyond the surface of these graphics.

Wayne chose lithography as the primary means to express the pulse of Donne's love poetry. During her first decade with this medium, she had come to feel that "it was a matter of love" between her and the stone. In lithography, her hand was actually on the delicate pores of the stone which took each line the way she meant it. When it re-acted in an unexpected way, she thought of this as a demonstration of the stone's life. By carefully observing and cultivating this "life," she became particularly attuned to the stone's potential, and carried her lithographic techniques to new heights of sophistication.

The first lithograph of the Donne project, "Shine here to us and thou art everywhere," from *The Sun Rising* (illus.) printed in October of 1956, uses the theme of *The Dreamers*, 1951 and 1952, animating it with new poetic contact. The heavenly fires which appear often in her Donne series, relate technically and visually to the climates of both the *Messenger* painting and the Fable series. Each was executed using natural materials. However, the galactic atmosphere is now deeper and the contrast between black and white, more intense. The figures also are related to earlier types. For example, the mushroom people in particular come to mind, although in "Shine here to us…" a new direction suggests amorphous bodies called from the heavens, not from drawing board modules or from symbolic fantasy. In this period, the modules are, in effect, points of light. The new type of figure drifts between the concept of the distant spheres and the sensuous immediacy of love's emotion, thereby suggesting a combination of dissimilar images. In her earlier work, she stressed certain parts of the bodies, most often a head or a hand. In her Donne work, the stress is often through abbreviated line.

This stone was printed to its natural border, as Wayne had done as early as 1951, to balance the

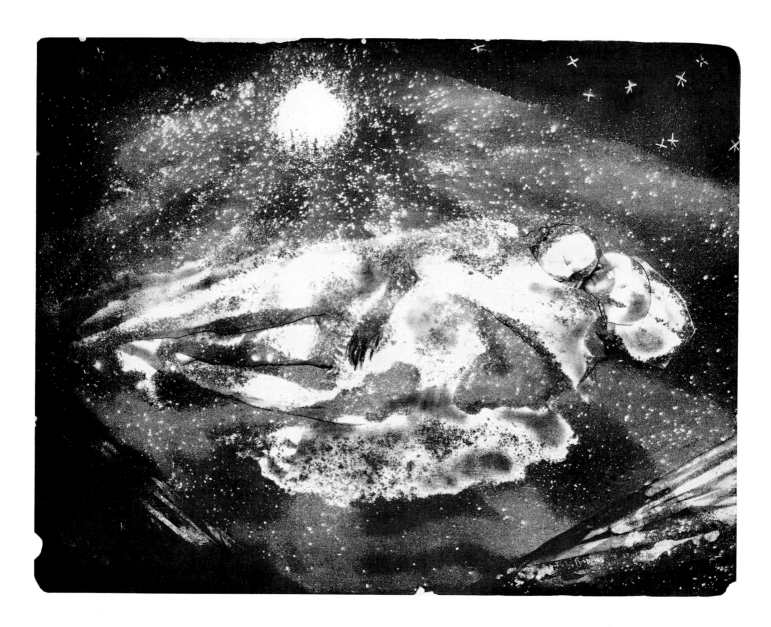

"Shine here to us and thou art everywhere," October, 1956; Donne Series; lithograph, 18⁵/₈ × 24⁵/₈"

"Whatever dies was not mixt equally," October, 1956; Crayon, pen, ink and wash, 19³/₄ × 25¹/₂";
Mr. and Mrs. Howard Elzer; Photo by Ik Serisawa

The Climb, 1957; lithograph,
$18^3/8 \times 14^1/4''$

cerebration of her image. The contradiction between the physical and the cerebral is especially poignant. The loving couple appears far removed from everyday reality, yet co-exists with the obvious, tangible border of the stone. It is a striking juxtaposition.

Of equal importance as an early work leading into the Donne ambiance is the drawing, "Whatever dyes was not mixt equally" from *The Good-Morrow* (illus.). The face in the lower right corner might be Wayne, brooding over the question posed by this Donne quote. The quote itself, is illustrated by the nudes who float above, over and through her mind. The body of the man with a mushroom cap is deteriorated by the black ink washes, suggesting the death in life which is love not equally given and received.

Alive with this imagery, and its potential in lithography, Wayne went to Paris in 1957 to work for two months with master-printer Marcel Durassier. Over half of the fourteen editions, several in more than one state, which Durassier pulled for her at this time, were inspired by lines or phrases of Donne's love poems. Other editions continued the theme of mushroom people *(The Climb)* (illus.), revealed her travels in France *(Hommage à Autun)* or were part of the exploratory "Monument series." "She is all States and all Princes, I," State II, from *The Sun Rising* (illus.) is among the most intense of the Donne images from these months: a man with an obvious mushroom cap and a woman, both figures flayed in their slenderness, entwine above a stone parapet.

"She is all States and all Princes, I," State II, 1957; Donne Series; lithograph, 25$^{1}/_{4}$ × 18$^{3}/_{4}$"

Working with Durassier allowed Miss Wayne to use European lithography techniques not feasible with Kistler. During these months, she began to do color lithographs, using primarily beige, blue, gray, green, and sanguine inks; she printed on handmade French papers unavailable in the United

The Canonization, 1958; from Songs and Sonets, John Donne; lithograph, $15 \times 11^{1}/_{8}''$

59

A Valediction: Forbidding Mourning, 1958;
from Songs and Sonets, John Donne; lithograph,
$15 \times 11^{1}/_{8}''$

States at that time and she incorporated tusche washes into her technical vocabulary. The execution of "She is all States..." reveals the sophistication of her techniques at this time:

"Liquid tusche applied with brush to coat the stone after which areas of tusche were wiped out with benzene and further drawing made with liquid tusche applied with brush and pen, tusche mixed with water puddled onto the stone and blown into, scraping with a razor blade."[32]

The following year, 1958, Wayne began etching in Los Angeles. Without a printer for her lithographs, she hoped that etching might be a possible course for the continuation of her graphics. However, the experience of making seven etchings proved that "etching is just not for me." To her mind, etching is too full of processes and therefore too slow; and because the acid actually creates the lines, she also felt that an etching could not bear her signature in the same personal way that a lithograph could.[33]

Therefore, in the fall of 1958, Wayne was back in Paris doing lithographs with Durassier again, intensely involved with Donne imagery, and intent now upon publishing a "livre de luxe" of the love poems. The result of a lithographic marathon which spanned the approximately seventy days and nights between October 15 and December 25, 1958 was the book, "John Donne, *Songs and Sonets,* Lithographs by June Wayne." Of the fifteen lithographs in the book, twelve were printed

in black and white and three in color. The edition numbered 110 (see Catalogue: Lithographs nos. 110–124). Each is printed to the deckle edges, "bleed image", on one half of a $15 \times 22^{1}/_{4}''$ sheet of Rives BFK paper which was then folded to enclose the poem.[34] The typographers were Brüder Hartmann of West Berlin, whose high standard of craftsmanship in graphic publication is evident in each carefully planned and executed detail. The images themselves, have power to change one's vision, to kindle a rethinking of the structure of the universe. They provide a powerful yet sensitive accompaniment to the poems.

The Canonization (illus.) was the first lithograph to be pulled. Tusche was sprayed with an airbrush over the bits of natural materials which Durassier quite appropriately called Miss Wayne's "cuisine." With its two taper-like figures burning from and into the heavenly fires of the atmosphere, the print image joins the poetic image to suggest a combination of death with life, life with death.

"We are tapers too, and at our own cost die..."

In the poem, a phoenix metaphor underscores this apparent union of opposites.

"The phoenix riddle hath more wit by us, ...
We die and rise the same, and prove mysterious by this love."

In the print Wayne stresses the same union by evoking figures to life from the non-being of heav-

The Relique, 1958, from Songs and Sonets,
John Donne; lithograph, 15 × 11¹/₈"
Two color: beige, black

enly fire only to allow them to withdraw visually into that fire again.

A Valediction: Forbidding Mourning (illus.) tackles Donne's famed compass image in which love's together-apart relation is made explicit.

"If they be two, they are two so as stiff twin compasses are two;
Thy soul, the fixed foot, makes no show to move, but doth if the other do.
And though it in the center sit, yet when the other far doth roam,
It leans and hearkens after it and grows erect as that comes home."

Although the print is only 15 × 11⅛", Wayne's image of two lovers is given its monumental scale by casting the figures into a starry field. Like the poem, the lithograph suggests a leaning together of the lovers and their erect apartness.

If "Shine here to us..." is thought to be the breakthrough print into the Donne context, *The Relique* (illus.) should be among those which mark the new directions of Wayne's work in the sixties. The technique by which the rocks in the background are textured, regulate the print's climate. This technique is further perfected in subsequent years. The organic patterns were executed with water-tusche washes on a zinc plate. Zinc, but not stone, will oxidize rapidly when exposed to air and moisture. This oxidation causes the wash to disperse into fractured lines and dots which can be printed. The resultant effect resembles the skin of a toad and therefore takes the French "peau de crapaud." Since this technique quite literally has its own "life" as it oxidizes, it appeals to Wayne who can direct the natural phenomenon to her purpose.

With the completion of the Donne book, Wayne began to concentrate on the problems of lithography, a craft which desperately needed to attract trained artisans into its ranks. This problem had been on her mind for a number of years. After working with Durassier, she had written to Gustave von Groschwitz, then Curator of Prints at the Cincinnati Art Museum, also a champion of fine lithography,

"I will rely largely on trips to Europe for my lithography in the future. It seems a long way to go to make a lithograph, but unless someone, somewhere realizes the straits this medium is in, it will have vanished with the present batch of printers."[35]

One "someone, somewhere" who would act creatively for the future of the medium, turned out to be June Wayne. In 1959, she wrote a plan to establish a lithography workshop where artisans could be trained for hand lithography in the United States. The Ford Foundation supplied the funds to carry out her proposal and in 1960, the creator of Donne images became the Director of this workshop, the Tamarind Lithography Workshop, Inc., Los Angeles.

The uniqueness of Tamarind is directly attributable to the fact that an artist designed the program and the artist was June Wayne. Her early experience on the WPA easel project informed her Tamarind thinking. She had liked the impersonal job category created for the artist at that time. As a result of her years of experience working with Lynton Kistler, she brought to Tamarind a special awareness of the economic pressures which are part of the problem of continuing a craft in an age of machines. Her background in industrial design, radio writing, sales, and diverse commercial endeavors, affected Tamarind's many facets. Perhaps her greatest asset, and certainly of most immediate importance in planning the workshop, was her experience from an artist's viewpoint in working with Durassier on the Donne lithographs. She felt that the two month rhythm of this experience was good timing for both printer and artist. When they parted, they left each other "on the upbeat." For this reason, Tamarind fellowship grants to artists for work with printers are for two months. From the long work hours with Marcel Durassier, she had also gained insight into the European craft structure which she could transpose in its best aspects or erase in its worst, to or from Tamarind. Following the "marvellous, exasperating, invigorating" experience of Donne's love poems as lithographic images in 1960, June Wayne "put herself aside as an artist" to do something for lithography.

The Lemmings 1960-1968

To June Wayne, who has "always been fascinated by lemmings," these oversized field mice that have an instinct for morbid togetherness and for periodic migrations leading to mass suicide, are a metaphor for people. In recent years she has brought literally thousands of "lemming people" onto the stage of her art work, directing them within the boundaries of her ideas about the content of her personal metaphor. She doesn't enjoy, for example, the zoologists' theories about the glands and genes which may regulate the lemmings' dramatic mass suicide. She wryly suggests that lemmings, like people, "merely elect someone who doesn't know the way."

In any case, the pure fancy which imbues her thinking about the still somewhat mysterious lemming is obvious, if the lemmings' particular relevance to her œuvre is not. The lemming as metaphor, however, like the mushroom, possesses the ambivalence and the combination of antitheses to be attractive to her. It is a dumb animal yet peculiarly human in its habits; repulsive as rodents are, but sympathetic. If at first erratic and timid in its migrations, marching under cover of night, it can also become mad with boldness, crashing upon any predator during broad daylight. Moreover, as the lemming people live in the environment of her lithographs, they become even more contrary as their frail, tiny scale is juxtaposed with the power of nature's cataclysms. Their delineated humanity clashes with the inhumanity of abstract surroundings.

Lemming people, although more detailed than in their guise of the sixties, first started to invade her work in the "Fable series" of 1955. In *Last Chance* (illus.) for example, crowds of these quite specifically textured lemming people are doing the same mindless things that people or lemmings might do. They quarrel, love, work and play; they seem always in nervous turmoil and they are always in groups. Other lithographs, *Walk on the Rocks*, 1964 and *Three Observers*, 1964 also show a preliminary interest in these figures, although not yet the feeling for the enormous crowds or for their clash with surroundings, both of which are part of Wayne's fully developed lemming metaphor.

A number of her Tamarind lithographs from 1965 to the present, those which belong to the fully

Last Chance, September, 1955; lithograph, 22¹/₂ × 28"

65

detail, actual size

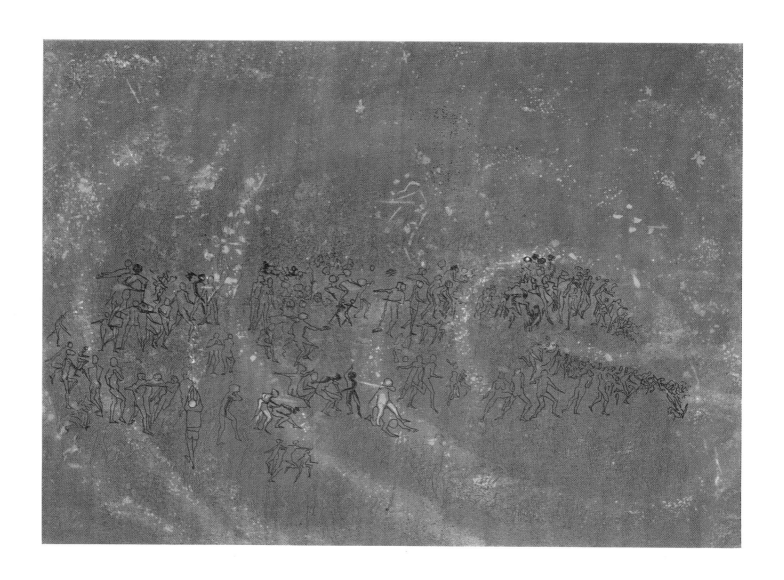

Lemmings Crush, May 8, 1967; Tamarind No. 2001; 21×30″, lithograph, bleed image

67

Tenth Memory, August 24, 1961
Tamarind No. 365; 30×22¹/₄″, lithograph,
bleed image

Dorothy the Last Day, August, 1960; Tamarind No. 107; 22¹/₄ × 30″, lithograph, bleed image

At Last a Thousand II, October 12, 1965; Tamarind No. 1000-B; lithograph, four color, 24×34"

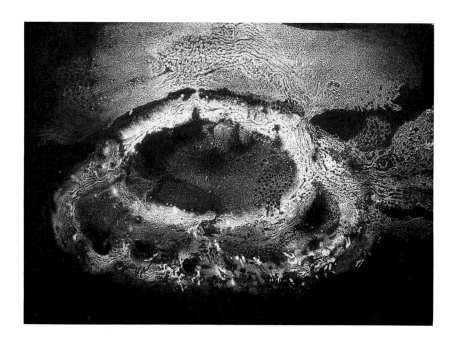

At Last a Thousand III, October 15, 1965
Tamarind No. 1000-C; lithograph, 24 × 34"
At Last a Thousand IV, October 18, 1965
Tamarind No. 1000-D; 24 × 29"

developed lemming statements, actually have lemming titles: *Lemmings Choice*, referring to a Party convention or an election; *Lemmings Crush* (illus.) referring to a mass crush of these figures falling over a cliff in a spiral of wildly colored space; *Lemmings Day*; *Lemmings Night*; and *Lemmings Twenty-One*. Other Lemming subjects disguised by their titles include: *At Last a Thousand*, *Two Thousand Too Soon*, *The Shelf*, *To Get to the Other Side*, *Plus ça change –*, and *Plus ça reste – même*.

Lemmings have been of increasing concern in Wayne's Tamarind lithographs although at the beginning she followed a "Memory series" (illus. *Tenth Memory*) and did occasional single themes (illus. *Dorothy the Last Day*). As director of the workshop, she has not had time for extended employment in her own behalf of the fine lithography facilities which are used by the artists-in-residence and by the guest artists. She has, more often, been at the press to experiment with, and develop, changing techniques and the requirements of their reflection in the printer's technology. These efforts have not, however, been a disadvantage since she has been freer to experiment with seeming impossibilities and to take risks with her work that another artist might be unwilling to undertake. Some of these trials have produced amazing new technical support for her images.

In two concentric circles suggesting a volcanic eruption around which the eye is directed, *At Last a Thousand* (illus.) communicates the immense scale of a natural catastrophe.[36] A wave in the cen-

The Shelf, September 27, 1967; Tamarind No.2003; lithograph, 18¹/₂ × 24"

tral core breaking against and over the top circle is as threatening as the patterned shape curving over the central area like a cyclone. *At Last a Thousand*, States III and IV, suggest a parade of lemming people on the perimeter of the lower circle, helplessly falling to their demise, and at the same time suggest revelers in a "Vassar daisy-

Stone Circle, May 15, 1967; Tamarind No. 2002; lithograph, 24 × 18¹/₂″

Lemmings Day, March 26, 1968; Tamarind No. 2195; lithograph, 20¹/₂ × 28″

Lemmings Day, March 26, 1968; Tamarind No. 2195; lithograph, $20^{1}/_{2} \times 28''$

To Get to the Other Side, January 29, 1968
Tamarind No. 2171; lithograph, 16 × 16¹/₂"

salt caused a dramatic oxidation for more pronounced, granular texturing. Wayne had accidentally discovered the effect of salt in washes on a zinc plate while working on *Twicknam Garden* for the Donne book in 1959. Now she intensifies its organic textures in an image which beautifully harmonizes with the technique's drama. After the salt particles were placed in the puddles of tusche, the mixture was allowed to dry for two days, resulting in a minutely cracked surface of visible oxidation. With an airbrush, from a distance of about two feet above the plate, the artist sprayed tusche over, not into, the plate, so that from a cloud of saturated air, the tusche gently floated down into the crevices of the oxide. This same zinc

chain." Wayne admits that had she wanted a specific reading, she would have made a more specific image. Here she establishes the climate, and puts the viewer on the "right continent", permitting him his personal reactions.

The four states of this lithograph (illus.) are four modifications of the emotional climate of the image while leaving its fundamental configuration intact. In State I, a black and white lithograph printed on zinc, she heightened the "peau de crapaud" effect, which was explained in relation to *The Relique* (illus.), by dropping salt particles into the water-tusche washes on the plate.[37] The

Lemmings Night, March 26, 1968; Tamarind No. 2238;
lithograph, three color; 21³/₄ × 28"

75

detail,
actual size

plate was printed in State II of the image after three aluminum plates, inked in tones of blue, orange and light green respectively, were run. The color state has a seductive, fire quality to it. State III, another black and white lithograph, is darker and thus more menacing than State I. The addition of inked solids and figures on the perimeter of the lower circle, and the deletion of border details with plate cleaner, account for the changes in this state. State IV is a shellac reversal of the key plate of the lithograph. It has the bleached quality of the first moment of intense light following an atomic explosion. To make white dominate this lithograph and reach its maximum intensity, the amount of black and gray had to be perfectly controlled. The narrowed format of this state is Miss Wayne's balancing factor.

Liquid tusche, sprayed over crumpled transfer paper and transferred to stone, gives to a number of Wayne's lithographs executed since 1967 a trompe l'oeil of rocky surfaces, of gigantic cloud banks and literally of the folded paper itself. *The Shelf* (illus.), a ledge of vertical rocks lit from behind the crevices, which was done in this manner, becomes the setting for a happening of lemming people. Sand was sprinkled into the tusche on the crumpled transfer paper of *Lemmings Day* (illus.) thereby granulating the lemming people's environment. In the small, square print *To Get To The Other Side* (illus.), she attempted the transfer of crumpled paper onto Mexican onyx rather than onto the traditional Bavarian limestone. After only four impressions were pulled the onyx cracked

and the edition had to be transferred to an aluminum plate in order to be completed. In this experiment it was evident, however, that onyx would provide a subtle and exciting surface for these transfers as well as for other lithographic techniques if the brittleness of that stone could be controlled.

Recently too, she has been using a positive-negative technique which requires a reversal of a plate or stone in the second run through the press, superimposed over the first run. Furthermore, if the second run is printed slightly off center, the textures "pop" as though lit from a side. Beginning with *Green Key*, 1963, Wayne developed this off center positive-negative technique until in *Lemmings Night*, 1968 (color plate) she achieved a tour de force expressing its remarkable potential. The resulting texture, which is again an environment for lemming people, is the soft gray-brown of night, in this case with the tactile and visual quality of worn, cut velvet. The nude figures placed toward the lower margin of the print are unaware of the imminent crests of enormous gray waves. The lemmings, then, are a current entry in June Wayne's personal lexicon from which she visually articulates her optical and kinetic concerns, her love for narrative and her philosophy of "discordant harmony."

A Summation in Sixti-Sexate 1959-September 20, 1968

The ranging scope and inexhaustible flexibility of June Wayne's art achieves yet another aspect in *Sixti-Sexate* (frontispiece) which looks like no other Wayne painting but is inescapably a Wayne.[38] Its sumptuous colors are made of organic, impasto-seeming modules arranged in optical and kinetic movement.

The surface of the canvas stimulates the eye in different ways, depending on whether one is seeing it close up, or from far, in flat daylight, or in sharp artificial light. Each change of distance and of light brings out a different dimension and each level of experience is inherent in the nature of the image.

The artist likes to have the painting seen at night, with an overhead raking light to emphasize the physical and trompe l'oeil ridges churning across the surface. She also likes diffuse light that emphasizes the graphic aspect of the colored modules "like an enormous woodcut." At sixty feet the painting has the look of moving water; close it appears brilliantly enameled and almost like an object of Art Nouveau.

The eyepath of *Sixti-Sexate* flows in a figure eight pattern reminiscent of the lithograph *Strange Moon* (illus.) In this case, however, the orbit moves around two diffusing multi-colored ovals of blue, green, violet and yellow. The white textures have a vertical rhythm, like a slim, breaking wave. One's eye follows the white movement of the surface, or the horizontal rocking of the colors, but not both at once. The artist refers to focal and peripheral transitions by painting the core of the color masses in more detail and intensified color than the periphery where she fades the color outward.

The painting's module is free form in appearance, the most amorphous-seeming unit she has used to date. But in fact it is a symbolic, biological module, like Adam and Eve's leaves (illus.) and is based on the rounded ovals of a layer of redwood bark.

"Somewhere in my supply of cuisine, I have a bag of redwood bark from the giant trees of Northern California. Its curious jigsaw puzzle shapes fascinate me. It looks so utterly machine-made, yet it grows as bark, fitting yin-yang into its neighbor in a marvellous intimacy."[39]

A module that appears man-made, but grows in one of the oldest trees known, was irresistible to the artist. She added the contradiction of turning solid redwood into a water reference in the way the modules bounce against each other and transmit a scintillating energy.

"I am seeking symbols and images, techniques and methods which will allow a picture to withstand the values and attrition of time. But always my intention is to move and illuminate..."[40]

Miss Wayne thinks of her technical means as tools to combat the attrition of time. Examples of her dedication to fine materials appear throughout the biography and text.
Thus in the painting *Sixti-Sexate* (frontispiece) Miss Wayne used a specially prepared 72×54" panel. Nine sheets of handmade all-rag paper, each approximately the same size as the canvas, were marouflaged to it with gesso plaster and gelatin.[41] The inevitable cracking of painted canvas is prevented because the paint has become one with its surface. Miss Wayne is doing a series on such panels which are already built and in her studio.
The artist's interest in the longevity of her aesthetic contrasts sharply with the vogue to substitute the act of creation for the art itself. Miss Wayne is not comfortable with this approach.

"It seems self-congratulatory. The artist becomes a has-been with press clippings that do not conform at all to the aging bore in one's presence. Beside, is it remarkable to make something that does not survive?"[42]

Miss Wayne intends that her work remain fresh as she made it, its subtle adjustment of emotion, content and structure constant in their relationship. She is aware that such a wish is meaningless in the face of time, particularly for "creatures with four score and ten years written into their genetic code." Even a hundred years seems a severe test for the survival of art works being made these days, but the artist admires the way man occasionally outwits his own limits "and becomes more human when he does." She enjoys making the limits dissolve; that there must be an end both to the individual and his work makes a temporary victory all the sweeter. June Wayne reports the suicide of the lemmings, but is not about to concede that the time, the place or the event is inevitable – even if it is.

NOTES TO THE TEXT

1 June Wayne, letter to the author, September 22, 1968.

2 Wayne, letter to Selden Rodman, April 13, 1956.

3 William S. Rubin, *Dada, Surrealism, and their Heritage*, New York, The Museum of Modern Art, 1968, pp. 20–21.

4 Wayne, tape recording to the author, August 3, 1968.

5 Tape recording of June Wayne lecture, University of New Mexico, March 23, 1968.

6 The symbolic shapes in the painting have suggested its classification with "Franz Kafka works." Obvious similarities between *The Cavern's* simple symbols and the more developed ones of *Kafka Symbols, Second Version* can be seen by comparing the former's statement of the mushroom and the latter's.

7 A striking comparison can be made between Wayne's *Strange Moon* of 1951 and Vasarely's black and white silkscreen *Vega* of 1957 (*Album III Cinétique*). Each has an individual approach to the optical excitement of black and white checks.

8 A by-product of *Strange-Moon* was the cover design for *Arts and Architecture*, February, 1951. This lithograph received Honorable Mention in an exhibition at the Denver Museum of Art in 1951.

9 Donald Bear, Director, Santa Barbara Museum of Art, June Wayne exhibition catalogue, March 15–31, 1950.

10 Wayne, tape recording to the author, August 19, 1968.

11 Wayne, letter to the author, September 16, 1968.

12 Wayne, tape recording to the author, August 15, 1968.

13 University of Illinois, *Contemporary American Painting*, 1951, pp. 222–223.

14 Wayne, tape recording to the author, August 15, 1968. This lithograph was the purchase prize from the exhibition, "Artists of Los Angeles and Vicinity," at the Los Angeles County Museum in 1950.

15 In 1950, the *Quiet One*, lithograph, received both a purchase prize and a first prize at the Los Angeles County Fair.

16 Jules Heller mistakenly wrote in *Printmaking Today* (1958) that the textures of this print were achieved with toothbrush splatter and scraped white lines. *The Witnesses* won the JHF Knoblock Prize for Lithography from the American Association of Graphic Artists 37th Annual Exhibition at Kennedy & Company, New York in 1953 and the purchase prize from the Pennell Fund for the Library of Congress in that same year.

17 Wayne, letter to the author, August 27, 1968.

18 Wayne, taped interview with author, July 26, 1968.

19 Ezra D. Ehrenkrantz, "Modular Materials and Design Flexibility," *Module, Proportion, Symmetry, Rhythm*, ed. Gyorgy Kepes, New York, George Braziller, Inc., 1966, pp. 118–127.

20 *Ibid.*, p. 118. Ehrenkrantz's comparison of a module and a musical keyboard is especially relevant here because of Miss Wayne's interest in and knowledge of music. She did, in fact, conceive of the paintings, *The Chase* and *The Elements* as "metaphors of fugues."

21 Wayne, letter to the author, September 16, 1968.

22 Wayne, letter to Donald Bear, January 8, 1951. This lithograph won honorable mention at the Los Angeles County Fair in 1951.

23 C. H. Waddington, "The Modular Principle and Biological Form," Kepes, *op. cit.*, pp. 20–37.

24 A certain dissatisfaction with the crystalline modules of this period might also explain the change of focus. Concerning the modules, the artist wrote in a letter to Peter Pollack, dated April 2, 1953, "I don't think that their influence on my direction of work will be more than temporary . . . because they are largely a seductive by-product of the same problems (i.e. aspects of optics) which are met more creatively in other, earlier works of mine. I am glad people like them, but can't afford to be taken in with my own poetry. Have been doing a whole lot of thinking ever since my show (The Pasadena Art Institute, November 30, 1952–January 4, 1953) and feel that whatever unique qualities I might have and whatever contributions I might make are likely to be in other directions . . . not so much in terms of 'feelings' as of conceptual ideas." Although not a published opinion, a segment of her public credited the works in memory of Donald Bear, executed in 1952 and 1953 (illus.), with the redirection of her focus out of the modules.

25 Wayne, letter to the author, September 16, 1968.

26 Wayne, letter to Pollack, (1955). *The Study for the Messenger*, both the painting and the lithograph, were the prize winners from this series. In 1955 the painting won a cash

award at the Laguna Beach Festival of Arts. The lithograph won honorable mention at the California State Fair in Sacramento in 1955 and the Mary S. Collins Prize at the Philadelphia Print Club, 28th Annual Exhibition of Lithography, 1956.

27 "Fables for the Undecided" is the artist's way of referring to Dr. Abraham Kaplan's untitled text and her illustrations for it.

28 Excerpts from Dr. Kaplan's unpublished manuscript are used in this text with their author's generous permission.

29 Kaplan, letter to Wayne, June 10, 1955.

30 Wayne, letter to Kaplan, June 17, 1955.

31 The prize-winners include: "Shine here to us...", purchase prize, San José State College, 1957, purchase prize, 1958 National Print Festival, Pasadena Art Museum; "Goe and catche a fallinge starre," purchase prize, Society of Washington Printmakers, 1958; "A winter-seeminge summer's night," purchase prize, Artists of Los Angeles and Vicinity, Los Angeles County Museum, 1958 and "This Extasie doth unperplex," purchase prize, Philadelphia Print Club, 1958. See Biography, 1959.

32 Documentation, Miss Donna Tryon, August 22, 1968.

33 A series of colored monotypes entitled "All day the same" from *The Extasie*, also date from this period. They were printed like Monet's haystacks had been painted, that is in many different color combinations to capture the colors of the atmosphere during different times of the day. See Catalogue: Monotypes, no. 167.

34 *The Extasie*, a three-color lithograph, is the one double page image in the book.

35 Wayne, letter to Gustave von Groschwitz, April 8, 1958.

36 *At Last a Thousand*, records the fact that Tamarind edition number 1000 was saved for the Director who was finally able, months after 1000 was reached in the chronological scheme, to find time to do it. Miss Wayne also liked the cataclysmic aura of the title which suited the image. Likewise, *Two Thousand Too Soon* refers to a Tamarind edition number. In this case, she created number 2000 before that number was reached. The title also hastens an end to our era.

37 Because a single grain of salt will affect an area of 4 to 5 square inches, a few dozen carefully placed grains were sufficient to get the textured effects of *At Last a Thousand*.

38 The artist chose the title *Sixti-Sexate* for this painting because it was started in 1960 and was completed in '68. Also she liked its quasi-ecclesiastical quality, particularly the sacred-profane tension in the last word.

39 Wayne, letter to the author, September 22, 1968.

40 Wayne, note by the artist, "New Talent in the U.S.," *Art in America*, XLV, March, 1957, p. 42.

41 Douglass Howell, the maker of these panels, is a world authority on the history and manufacture of handmade paper. His private mill is located in Westbury, Long Island.

42 Wayne, note to author, October 10, 1968.

A Biographical Sketch

To understand the art of June Wayne, it is important to know something about the forces and events which shaped her early life.

She was raised in Chicago during the 20's and 30's in neighborhoods described by James T. Farrell in *Studs Lonigan*, and by Saul Bellow in *The Adventures of Augie March*. These neighborhoods overflowed with first generation Americans struggling to gain an economic foothold in a society still burdened by sweatshops. The early days of the labor movement, flappers, prohibition, gangsters, the St. Valentine's Day massacre, and the Depression make up the climate of her early childhood memories. The steel mills of Gary, Indiana, where she lived briefly with her mother and grandparents, figure in many of her 1935–1940 paintings.

Born March 7, 1918, the only child of Albert and Dorothy Alice (née Kline) La Vine, she scarcely knew her father since her parents were divorced when she was a baby. Her mother went to work to support herself and infant daughter. By 1924, the three generations, widowed grandmother, divorcée mother and the small girl were well aware that outside their door was a hostile and dangerous world. Although money was not a desperate problem, it was sufficiently serious so that the importance of learning to support oneself was clear to June at an early age.

Despite the uncertainties of the Depression, an atmosphere of culture and intellectual curiosity prevailed at home. June and her mother were both voracious readers, and setting a pattern in which she learned things her own way, she taught herself to play the piano by ear. At the age of 5 she made a discovery which was integral to her later interest in problems of painting as influenced by optics. She observed that the dots of color in the comic strips, when fused by vision, produced secondary hues. Thus she unknowingly shared a fundamental technical premise with the art of the French Impressionist. Even then she thought of herself as an artist and executed many drawings composed entirely of colored dots.

At 9, June began to paint an illuminated manuscript of the *Rubáiyat of Omar Khayyam*, a project that occupied her attention into her late teens. This manuscript was the first expression of her love for painting, poetry and books. It also represented the ability to undertake a complex project and carry it on for years, a quality that imbued her directorship of the Tamarind Lithography Workshop many years later.

She did well in grammar school, skipping several grades, and entered Senn High School. However, her interest in organized education rapidly declined. Bored and restless, she began spending days, even weeks, at a time, at the Clark Street Branch of the Public Library. During the third year of high school, she dropped out of Senn. Later to prove to her mother that she was well educated despite lack of a high school diploma, she took and passed entrance examinations to the University of Chicago in 1934 when she was sixteen. Instead of entering college, she left home and began supporting herself with a series of factory jobs. Nevertheless she lived near the campus and soon

Wayne at her drawing table
in the studio at 1108 N.
Tamarind Avenue

82

became a part of university life. She travelled in a milieu of scientists, artists and writers that included Abe Aaron, Nelson Algren, Saul Bellow, James T. Farrell, Meyer Levin and Richard Wright. She formed a particularly meaningful friendship with a research chemist, Harold Jacobson, who was intrigued by her precocity and challenged her to probe many intellectual ideas she had not as yet explored. Jacobson also introduced her to Franz Kafka's works, to the Beethoven late quartets, and to his favorite thesis that "nothing is as it seems." In 1935, at the age of 17, she received her first pro-

fessional recognition with a one-man show of paintings at the Boulevard Gallery in Chicago. She signed her works with her first and middle names, June Claire.

As a result of that show, she received an invitation from the Department of Public Education of the Mexican Government to paint in Mexico. She produced an exhibition which opened in October, 1936, at the Palacio de Bellas Artes, Mexico City. After this show, which was well received, she returned to Chicago. Still faced with the need to earn her living, she took a job in the art galleries of Marshall Field and Company, 1937–38. Her duties included hanging exhibitions, selling pictures, and if necessary, dusting the stock. In this way she got a close look at the difference between the picture business and the art business – a distinction that proved valuable to the Tamarind program two decades later.

The following year, 1938, she became involved with the easel painting project of the Illinois WPA Federal Art Project. Her paintings, executed in palette knife strokes of broken color, were social comments and expressionistic in style.

June Claire became a familiar figure in the Artist's Union. On behalf of her colleagues she successfully lobbied in Washington, D.C. against a congressional amendment to discharge WPA artists every sixteen weeks. Her friends were the artists of the period among whom were Julio de Diego, Arthur Lidov, Sidney Loeb, Edward Millman, Mitchell Siporin, Bernard Rosenthal and Emerson Woelffer; also Peter Pollack, head of the WPA Art Centers. In 1939 she was offered her first significant job, as a jewelry designer-stylist in New York City. She travelled the New England jewelry factory circuit, producing ornaments in metal, wood, leather, glass and imitation stones. These costume jewelry designs were for mass production, and during this period she learned the techniques of rapid decision-making, and of costing out her ideas so that they were practical to manufacture and to sell. However, she continued to paint and exhibit in group shows until, in 1941, she met and married George Jerome Wayne, M.D. Shortly thereafter he was sent as a flight surgeon to the Burma-India theatre of war.

In 1942 she was hit by a bad bout of rheumatic fever at the same time that scarcity of metals displaced her job. She decided to leave New York and go to California. Her painting was too physically strenuous for her, so she enrolled in a course in production illustration given by the California Institute of Technology in conjunction with the Art Center School of Los Angeles. The techniques she acquired were significant to her later work in optics. At the same time she taught herself to write for radio, and in 1943 joined the staff of WGN in Chicago writing music continuity and war effort programs.

In 1944, Dr. Wayne returned from overseas and a daughter, Robin Claire, was born in California on December 8. For all of 1945, the Waynes lived in Army towns, travelling by car and trailer in nomadic fashion. In 1946, after Dr. Wayne was discharged from the service, they settled permanently in Los Angeles.

Among the new friends they made was Jules Langsner, a psychiatric social worker who subsequently became an internationally known art critic. Langsner had been, since childhood, an intimate of Jackson Pollack, Philip Guston and Ruben Kadish, all of whom were from California. His encyclopedic command of art history was immensely interesting to June Wayne. Furthermore at this time Langsner was developing his own theories of the interrelatedness of science and art; thus he was fascinated by her ideas about optics, symbols and the potential for narrative within a new configurational structure.

Self portrait, 1947; Oil on canvas, 20×16"
An experiment using two focal areas, the left and right eye,
with intervening peripheral optical distortions

From 1947 to 1950 she produced many of the experiments which, even now, are ahead of the times.
It was during this period that she searched out Lynton Kistler and began their long collaboration to produce lithographs through 1956. At Kistler's workshop she met artist Clinton Adams. She

admired his command of the medium, and he became her associate at Tamarind years later. During the years, 1942 to 1950, she was indifferent to and isolated from the world of museums, publicity and exhibitions, but in 1950, after an exhibition gap of 11 years, Donald J. Bear, Director of the Santa Barbara Museum of Art, arranged a one-man exhibition of her paintings, constructions and lithographs, most of which were sold. Many of those works later were loaned for a show at the Pasadena Art Museum for which, in 1952, the Los Angeles Times named her Woman of the Year for Meritorious Achievement in Modern Art. At just about the same time, June Wayne broke her years of isolation and joined with William Brice, Jules Langsner, John Entenza, Rico Lebrun, Henry Seldis and other prominent members of the Los Angeles art community to fight for, and win, a retraction of a City Council resolution labeling modern artists as "tools of the Kremlin." This was an act of courage in those days of intense Joseph McCarthy anti-intellectualism, and shifted the official climate of Los Angeles into one much more hospitable to its artists.

In 1953, Wayne participated in yet another activity of the art world by becoming a consultant to the discussion series *You and Modern Art*, developed by Jules Langsner for the Fund for Adult Education of the Ford Foundation.

1954 and 1955 were dedicated to her work. She saw an exceptional lithograph by the Monegasque artist, Mario Avati; it was *La Métropolitaine* owned by the Museum of Modern Art in New York. She determined to locate the master-printer who had pulled it because the quality of the washes was exceptional, and beyond the technical range of her Kistler oeuvre. She began a search for Avati, located him in Paris, and in 1957 thanks to Avati, Marcel Durassier began to work with her. She was already involved with her visual metaphors for the poetry of John Donne, and with Durassier she produced an impressive body of works, adding European techniques to her own repertoire in lithography.

1958 found her back in California, still absorbed in the Donne images. Feeling it was time to attempt a "livre de luxe" on Donne, in October of 1958 she returned to Paris to create the book.

June Wayne drawing on stone, 1965, in her studio at 1112 N. Tamarind Avenue, in Hollywood. This is one of a cluster of three buildings in which she lives and works

She returned to Los Angeles in January of 1959 amid widespread critical acclaim:

"It is to June Wayne's eternal credit that she has undertaken the heroic task of 'setting' some of the lines of John Donne to 'visual music' and thus become one of the first American artists to illustrate a great poet . . . the whole has resulted in a new triumph for the contemporary art of the book."

EBRIA FEINBLATT, Curator of Prints and Drawings, Los Angeles County Museum of Art.

"June Wayne a ce qu'il faut (imagination et technique) pour nous donner par l'image une équivalence de la poésie du grand Anglais."

PIERRE COURTHION, Paris.

The Donne book was acquired by many museums, libraries and private collectors, and several exhibitions of her drawings, etchings and lithographs took place. About this time, 1959, she acquired a large studio at 1112 N. Tamarind Avenue, Los Angeles. Still engrossed in lithography, and worried about its moribund condition in the United States, she wrote an imaginative but unorthodox plan for W. McNeil Lowry, Director of the Ford Foundation's Program in Humanities and the Arts. This plan was a blueprint for how lithography could be restored through the systematic recreation of master-printers to work with U.S. artists.

1960 was a year of public success and private loss. The Ford Foundation granted $165,00 for a test

The artist at her desk, November, 1968
Photo by Daniel Ross

first lithograph she produced in the Tamarind program, *Dorothy the Last Day* (illus.). Her grandmother died shortly thereafter. Also she divorced Dr. Wayne the same year.

When the Ford grant came through, she was in the middle of painting *Sixti-Sexate* (frontispiece) but the demands of the workshop were acute and the painting was not completed until eight years later. She did, however, continue creating lithographs although, paradoxically, not as prolifically as would have been the case had the workshop been less successful. In 1962, the Ford Foundation granted another $400,000 to enlarge the Tamarind program, and in 1965 a third grant of $900,000 funded it into 1970.

Since its start, more than 150 artists from the United States and abroad have worked at Tamarind, and its reputation for excellence is widespread. The City Council of Los Angeles, which she fought so bitterly in the early 50's, honored her in 1962 for her leadership of the Tamarind Lithography Workshop. She also was elected to the Board of Directors of the Grunwald Graphic Arts Foundation at the University of California at Los Angeles; then she was appointed to the National Committee of the Department of State, Art in the Embassies Program.

Late in 1964, June Wayne married Arthur Henry Plone. Together they went to Europe early in 1965 because she wanted to persuade European papermakers to improve the quality and increase the quantity of handmade papers for lithography. At this time the supply of paper was being severely

of her plan. On July 1, Tamarind Lithography Workshop opened, with June Wayne as Director, Clinton Adams as Associate Director, and Garo Antreasian as Technical Director. But that same week, her mother died, an event revealed in the

diminished because world-wide inflation attracted the paper mills to the lucrative bank-note business. She was successful in impressing them with their responsibility to art and artists, and the all-rag paper basic to the maintenance of Tamarind's standard of quality again began to be available in the United States.

In 1967 she wrote *"Operation Cornerstone,"* a proposal that the National Endowment in the Arts develop an Office of Material Resources for the Fine Arts, to protect and monitor the quality of materials needed by artists. The shortage of lithograph stones, handmade paper and stable, lightfast inks worries her. She was not able to attract support for Operation Cornerstone, but still hopes her plan will become feasible one day.

In 1967 she became a trustee of the National Citizens Committee for Public Television, a responsibility she still holds.

In September of 1967, Jules Langsner died. This was recorded in her cryptic lithograph *Thirteenth Memory* which has not been released either for sale or exhibition.

Early in 1968, June Wayne established the Stone Circle Foundation, a tax-exempt organization devoted to the original print. Its name echoes the mystery of Stonehenge, but it also refers to the circle of artists and artisans who, like herself, love the beauty of the lithograph stone. In June of 1968, she moved into the enlarged studio which she designed herself and had built at 1108 N. Tamarind Avenue. She has completed *Sixti-Sexate* and is preparing a new series of paintings. When asked what she had in mind for the next creative step, Miss Wayne replied, "This seems a time to gift you with my uncommon silence."

CATALOGUE

Dimensions of each work are given in inches, height before width. Starred numbers are illustrated in the text.

PARTIAL LIST OF EXTANT PAINTINGS

1 Untitled (Mexican woman wearing rebozo), 1936; Oil on canvas, 25³/₄ × 19³/₄; Collection of the Artist

2 Waiting for Newspapers, 1936; Oil on canvas, 25 × 22; Collection of the Artist

Paintings done while on the easel project of the Illinois WPA Federal Art Project, Chicago, 1938; Whereabouts unknown

3 Self-Portrait, 1947; Oil on canvas, 20 × 16; Collection of the Artist

*4 Cavern, 1948; Oil on canvas, 35 × 54; Collection of the Artist (Illus. p. 13)

5 Cryptic Creatures, December, 1948; Oil on canvas, 36 × 30; Collection of the Artist

6 Moving Symbols, 1948; Oil on canvas, 36 × 30; Mrs. Jules Langsner

7 Witching Hour, 1948; Oil on canvas, 40 × 30; Mrs. Jules Langsner

*8 The Chase, February 28, 1949; Oil on canvas, 20 × 80; Collection of the Artist (Illus. p. 21)

9 The Hero, December 13, 1949; Oil on canvas, 40 × 30; Dr. and Mrs. Leonard Rosengarten

10 Night Swim, 1949; Oil on canvas, 10 × 60; Herbert W. Lerner

*11 The Quiet One, June 20, 1949; Oil on canvas, 30 × 14; Dr. and Mrs. Leonard Rosengarten (Illus. p. 26)

12 Sad Flute Player, 1949; Oil on canvas, 20 × 16; Dr. Aerol Arnold

13 The Tunnel, 1949; Oil on canvas, 25 × 30; Mrs. Harry J. Lackritz

Note: The Tunnel, oil painting of 1947, has been destroyed by the artist.

14 The Dark One, June 7, 1950; Oil on canvas, 60 × 28; Collection of the Artist

*15 Fireworks, 1950; Oil on canvas, 30 × 30; Mrs. Mathilda Barlow (Illus. p. 14)

16 The Ladder, June, 1950; Oil on canvas, 60 × 28; Collection of the Artist

17 Mushroom People, 1950; Oil on canvas, 24 × 20; Dr. and Mrs. Milton Miller

18 The Witnesses, 1950; Oil on canvas, 20 × 24; Herbert W. Lerner

*19 The Elements, 1951; Oil in wax on canvas, 27 × 90; Collection of the Artist (Illus. p. 22)

20 The Law Court, 1951; Oil on canvas, 36 × 50; Estate of Albert E. Lewin

*21 The Sanctified, 1951; Oil in wax on canvas, 40 × 30; Mr. and Mrs. Benjamin B. Smith (Illus. p. 33)

22 The Advocate, September 8, 1952; Oil on canvas, 60 × 28; Collection of the Artist

*23 The Dreamers, 1952; Oil on canvas, 21 × 63; Dr. and Mrs. Lyman Harrison (Illus. p. 36)

24 Strange Moon, 1952; Oil on canvas, 16 × 20; Mrs. Celia Coit

25–27. Triptych, c. 1952

25 The Advocate (center panel); Oil on canvas, 36 × 18; Dr. and Mrs. Lester Morrison

26 The Bride (right panel); Oil on canvas, 36 × 18; Mr. and Mrs. Douglas Honnold

27 The Suitor (left panel); Oil on canvas, 36 × 18; Mr. and Mrs. Douglas Honnold

28 The Awakened, 1953; Oil on canvas, 36 × 54; Dr. Benjamin Jurin

29 Study for the Messenger, April, 1954; Oil on canvas, 20 × 60; Collection of the Artist

30 Study for the Messenger, March, 1955; Oil on canvas, 30×36; Collection of the Artist

*31 The Messenger, 1955; Oil on canvas, 60×50; Collection of the Artist (Illus. p. 41)

*32 The Saint and the Sinner, April, 1956; Oil on canvas, 20×60; Collection of the Artist (Illus. p. 50)

33 The Witnesses, July, 1956; Oil on canvas, 50×60; Collection of the Artist

*34 Sixti-Sexate, September 20, 1968; Oil on paper maroufleged onto canvas with gesso and gelatin, 72×54; Collection of the Artist (Illus. p. 2)

PARTIAL LIST OF EXTANT DRAWINGS

Each drawing except number 35 is signed, titled and dated by the artist.

35 Study for Quiet One (Lithograph), 1949; Crayon, pen and ink, 20³/4×12¹/4; Collection of the Artist

36 The Assayer, 1952; Crayon, pen and ink, 38¹/4×25¹/2; Dr. and Mrs. Alex Rogawski

37 The Awakened, 1952; Pencil, crayon, pen and ink, 52¹/2×35¹/2; Whereabouts unknown

38 Study for the Bride, 1952; Pencil, crayon, pen and ink, 35¹/2×52; Dr. Benjamin Jurin

39 A Work of Mourning for Donald Bear, 1952; Crayon, pen and ink, 24¹/2×25¹/2; Whereabouts unknown

40 First Version of the Travellers, June, 1954; Crayon, ink spray, pen and ink, 22×30¹/8; Collection of the Artist

41 Study for the Messenger, August, 1954; Crayon and tusche spray, 26×19⁷/8; Collection of the Artist

*42 Third Study for the Messenger, November, 1954; Ink spray, pen and ink, 12³/4×10; Collection of the Artist (Illus. p. 42)

43 First Study for Tower of Babel, June 25, 1955; Crayon and ink spray, 29×23¹/8; Collection of the Artist

44 Fifth Study for the Sinner, 1956; Crayon, ink spray, pen and ink, 22¹/4×28; Collection of the Artist

45 (On hearing a discussion of Bosch, June 27, 1956), The Man with the White Eye, August 27, 1956; Crayon, ink spray, pen and ink over discarded lithography proof, 26¹/4×20¹/4; Collection of the Artist

*46 "Whatever dies was not mixt equally", October, 1956; Crayon, pen, ink and wash, 19³/4×25¹/2; Mr. and Mrs. Howard Elzer (Illus. p. 55)

47 "I long to talk," April 27, 1958; Crayon, pen, ink and wash, 20×15¹/2; Mr. and Mrs. Jules Kaplan

48 "Make me a mandrake — or a stone fountain," 1958; Pen, ink and wash, 20⁵/8×15⁷/8; Dr. and Mrs. Leonard Asher

49 XIXth Elegie, 1958; Crayon, pen, ink and wash, 22¹/8×29⁷/8; Arthur H. Plone

50 "Oh more than moon," 1958; Crayon, pen, ink and wash, c. 24×32; Dr. Benjamin Jurin

51 The Relique, 1958; Crayon, Chinese white, pen, ink and wash, 12×31⁷/8; Collection of the Artist

52 "Send back my heart and eyes," June, 1958; Crayon, pen, ink and wash, 30×22¹/4; Collection of the Artist

53 The Sunne Rising I, 1958; Crayon, ink spray, pen and ink, 12³/8×9¹/2; Collection of the Artist

54 "Whoever comes to shroud me," 1958; Pen, ink and wash, 15¹/4×22¹/8; Collection of the Artist

55 "Who is so safe as wee," 1958; Crayon, pen, ink and wash, 30×22¹/4; Mr. and Mrs. James L. Hill

Dimensions of the printed area are given in inches, height before width. The edition noted is the numbered artist's edition which excludes printer's and artist's proofs. Unless otherwise noted, lithographs are printed in black and white. Detailed documentation on techniques and extant proofs is in the possession of the artist. The use of an image on a stone or metal plate in more than one edition, a characteristic of the artist's lithographs, is noted in the documentation.

Lynton R. Kistler printed each lithograph executed through 1956. Other printers are noted accordingly.

56 The Cavern #1, June, 1948; $9^7/_{16} \times 13^5/_{16}$; Edition: 35

57 Kafka Symbol #1, July, 1948; $13^7/_8 \times 17^1/_2$; Edition: 32

58 Black Ball in a Room, October, 1948; $14^3/_4 \times 18$; Edition: 30; One-color: Brownish black
Note: Black Ball in a Room is predecessor to The Target.

*59 Kafka Symbols Second Version, February, 1949; $27^3/_4 \times 21^3/_4$; Edition: 30 (Illus. p. 21)

60 The Tunnel #1, June, 1949; $13^7/_8 \times 17^1/_4$; Edition: 25

*61 The Hero, December, 1949; $27^1/_2 \times 21^3/_4$; Edition: 33 (Illus. p. 24)

*62 Quiet One, January, 1950; $20^5/_8 \times 11^{15}/_{16}$; Edition: 33 (Illus. p. 27)

63 The Sad Flute Player, January, 1950; $16^5/_{16} \times 13^3/_8$; Edition: 30

*64 The Retreat, April, 1950; $13^{15}/_{16} \times 20^1/_8$; Edition: 35 (Illus. p. 25)

*65 The Sanctified, December, 1950; $13^3/_4 \times 17^7/_8$; Edition: 35 (Illus. p. 32)

*66 The Cavern #2, January, 1951; $21^1/_4 \times 29^1/_8$; Edition: 35 (Illus. p. 12)

*67 Strange Moon, February, 1951; $13^7/_8 \times 18^1/_8$; Edition: 35 (Illus. p. 15)

*68 The Target, February, 1951; $14^1/_{16} \times 17^7/_8$; Edition: 35 (Illus. p. 18)

*69 The Tunnel #2, July, 1951; $15^1/_2 \times 19^5/_8$; Edition: 35 (Illus. p. 17)

*70 The Bride, December, 1951; $27^1/_2 \times 7^7/_8$; Edition: 35 (Illus. p. 34)
Note: Printed simultaneously with no. 71 on a single sheet of paper and cut into separate lithographs after printing.

*71 The Suitor, December, 1951; $27^1/_2 \times 7^7/_8$; Edition: 35 (Illus. p. 34)

*72 The Advocate, January, 1952; $27^1/_2 \times 7^7/_8$; Edition: 35 (Illus. p. 34)

73 The Dreamers, January, 1952; $8^7/_8 \times 29^3/_8$; Edition: 35
Note: The Suitor, left panel; The Advocate, middle panel; The Bride, right panel of triptych. The Dreamers, frieze above triptych.

74 The Witnesses I, September, 1952; $22^7/_8 \times 28^3/_4$; Edition: 27

 * The Witnesses II, First Version; Edition: 14 (Illus. p. 28)
The Witnesses II, Second Version; Edition: 15

75 The Witnesses #2, September, 1952; $9 \times 11^1/_2$; Edition: 25

76 The Hunter, October, 1952; $12^5/_8 \times 9^3/_4$; Edition: 38

*77 A Work of Mourning III, February, 1953; Donald Bear Series; $31^3/_4 \times 24$; Edition: 30 (Illus. p. 40)

78 A Work of Mourning IV, February, 1953; Donald Bear Series; $20 \times 13^3/_4$; Edition: 30

79 The Curious, July, 1953; $14^3/_4 \times 18^3/_8$; Edition: 30

80–85 Justice Series

*80 The Jury, September, 1953; $18 \times 14^3/_4$; Edition: 14 (Illus. p. 42)

81 Second Jury, December, 1953; $11^3/_4 \times 15^5/_8$; Edition. 25

*82 Final Jury, January, 1954; $23^1/_4 \times 32$; Edition: 30 (Illus. p. 43)

*83 The Travellers, August, 1954; 25¹/₄×18¹/₂; Edition: 35 (Illus. p. 44)

84 Study for a Messenger IV, December, 1954; 15³/₄×11⁷/₈; Edition: 35

*85 Study for a Messenger V, January, 1955; Offset lithograph; 18⁷/₈×26; Edition: 35 (Illus. p. 45)

86–91 Fable Series, Offset lithographs

86 Study for the Wing of the Devil, May, 1955; 25×19; Edition: 60

*87 The First Critic, July, 1955; 26⁷/₈×19; Edition: 100 (Illus. p. 48)

*88 Tower of Babel A, August, 1955; 26⁷/₈×19¹/₄; Edition: 100 (Illus. p. 49)

*89 Last Chance, September, 1955; 22¹/₂×28; Edition: 100. (Illus. p. 64/65)

90 Tower of Babel B, September, 1955; 27×20¹/₂; Edition: 100

91 Tower of Babel C, September, 1956; 21¹/₄×18⁵/₈; Edition: 225

*92 "Shine here to us and thou art everywhere," October, 1956; Donne Series; 18⁵/₈×24⁵/₈; Edition: 25 (Illus. p. 54)

93 The Start of a Rock, December, 1956; 15⁷/₈×11⁷/₈; Edition: 18

Nos. 94–107 were printed in Paris by Marcel Durassier

94 The Anniversarie, 1957; Donne Series; 20⁵/₈×16³/₈; Edition: 35; Two-color: reddish brown, black

*95 The Climb, 1957; 18³/₈×14¹/₄; Edition: 20 (Illus. p. 56)

96 First Monument – Paris, 1957; 22×16¹/₈; Edition: 35

97 "Goe and catche a falling starre," 1957; Donne Series; 13¹/₂×17³/₄; Edition: 35; Three-color: light green, grey, black

98 Hommage à Autun, 1957; 26³/₈×15¹/₄; Edition: 30
Color States:
Hommage à Autun II; Edition: 15; Two-color: dark blue, light tan

Hommage à Autun III; Edition: 15; Two-color: brown, light tan

99 Monument II – Paris, May, 1957; 11³/₄×15⁵/₈; Edition: 28

100 "She is all States and all Princes, I," State I, 1957; Donne Series; 25¹/₄×18³/₄; Edition: 12
* "She is all States and all Princes, I," State II; Edition: 24 (Illus. p. 57)

101 Third Monument – Paris, 1957; 14×18¹/₂; Edition: 25

102 "This Extasie doth unperplex," 1957; Donne Series; 14³/₄×19³/₄; Edition: 25; Three-color: pale blue, beige, sanguine
"This Extasie doth unperplex II;" Edition: 25; Three-color: pale blue, beige, black

103 "Two graves hide thine and my course," 1957; Donne Series; 16³/₈×21⁵/₈; Edition: 30

104 "We are Tapers, too," 1957; Donne Series; 20¹/₂×16³/₈; Edition: 35; Two-color: blue, black

105 "We must leave at last in Death," 1957; Donne Series; 14³/₄×21³/₈; Edition: 25

106 "A winter-seeming summer's night," 1957; Donne Series; 16×21³/₄; Edition: 35

107 "Yesternight the Sunne went hence," 1957; Donne Series; 15¹/₂×21¹/₄; Edition: 12

*108 Adam en attente, 1958; Offset lithograph; 31¹/₂×9¹/₂. Printer: Lynton R. Kistler (Illus. p. 37)
Printed simultaneously with no. 109 in all three editions on single sheets of paper and cut into separate lithographs after printing.
First Edition: 90
Note: White wove paper.
Second Edition: 60
Note: Grey laid paper
Third Edition: 50
Note: Beige wove paper

*109 Eve tentée, 1958; Offset lithograph; 31¹/₂×9¹/₂. Printer: Lynton R. Kistler. (Illus. p. 37)
First Edition: 90

Note: The apples and Eve's "mushroom" in some impressions in each edition were hand tinted in rose. See no. 108 for explanation of different editions.
Second Edition: 60
Third Edition: 50

Nos. 110–132 were printed in Paris by Marcel Durassier

110–124 Songs and Sonets by John Donne, December 25, 1958; Livre de luxe; Each single page image, 15 × 11¹/₈; The double page image (The Extasie), 15 × 22¹/₄; Edition: 110
Dimensions of these and other sheets of handmade and/or handtorn paper vary slightly.

110 Hexastichon Bibliopolae

111 The Good Morrow

112 Song. Three-color: pale blue, black, sanguine

113 The Sunne Rising

*114 The Canonization (Illus. p. 58)

115 The Breake of Day

116 The Anniversarie

117 Twicknam Garden

118 A Valediction: Of Weeping

119 The Baite

120 The Apparition

*121 A Valediction: Forbidding Mourning (Illus. p. 59)

122 The Funerall

123 The Extasie; Three-color: light grey-blue, light olive-green, sanguine

*124 The Relique; Two-color: beige, black (Illus. p. 61)

125 Two Graves – III Version, 1958; Donne Series; 10⁵/₈ × 14³/₈; Edition: 20

126 Les Amants, 1959; 15 × 22¹/₄, bleed image; 4 proofs

127 Lava Bed, January, 1959; 15¹/₈ × 22³/₄; Edition: 25

128 Memory of a Tanagra – The Man, State I, 1959; 22¹/₄ × 15¹/₄; Edition: 15

Color States:

Memory of a Tanagra – The Man, State II; Edition: 10; Three-color: yellow, pink, black
Memory of a Tanagra – The Man, State II, Second Version; Edition: 15; Three-color: pink, yellow, black
Memory of a Tanagra – The Man, State III; Edition: 6; Three-color: beige, green, black
Memory of a Tanagra – The Man, State IV; Edition: 5; Three-color: blue, green, black
Memory of a Tanagra – The Man, State V; Edition: 10; Three-color: dark yellow, light yellow, black
Memory of a Tanagra – The Man, State VI; Edition: 10; Two-color: beige, blue
Memory of a Tanagra – The Man, State VII; Edition: 10; Three-color: blue, turquoise, black

129 Memory of a Tanagra – The Woman, State I, 1959; 22¹/₄ × 15¹/₈; Edition: 15

Color States:

Memory of a Tanagra – The Woman, State II; Edition: 10; Three-color: pink, yellow, black
Memory of a Tanagra – The Woman, State II, Second Version; Edition: 5; Three-color: yellow, pink, black
Memory of a Tanagra – The Woman, State III; Edition: 6; Three-color: green, beige, black
Memory of a Tanagra – The Woman, State IV; Edition: 5; Three-color: green, blue, black
Memory of a Tanagra – The Woman, State V; Edition: 10; Three-color: dark yellow, light yellow, black
Memory of a Tanagra – The Woman, State VI; Edition 10; Two-color: beige, blue
Memory of a Tanagra – The Woman, State VII; Edition: 10; Three-color: turquoise, blue, black

130 Memories of Things to Come I, 1959; 15³/₈ × 11³/₈; Edition: 30

131 Memory of Things to Come II, 1959; 26¹/₂ × 15¹/₄; Edition: 30

Color State:

Memory of Things to Come II, State II; Edition: 11; Two-color: tan, dark blue

132 The Wall, 1959; 21¹/₄×17; 4 unique proofs

For each of the following editions that bears a Tamarind number, there is a "Tamarind edition" of nine impressions in addition to the artist's edition noted below.

*133 Dorothy the Last Day, August, 1960; Tamarind No. 107; 22¹/₄×30, bleed image; Edition: 20; Printer: Garo Antreasian; Four-color: pale blue-grey, pale olive-green, light tan, dark brown (Illus. p. 68)

134 Cornelia's Bird, September 8, 1960; Tamarind No. 107 A; 22¹/₄×30, bleed image; Edition: 20; Printer: Garo Antreasian

135 Spectator, November 3, 1960; Tamarind No. 143; 30× 22¹/₄, bleed image; Edition: 10: designated A–J plus 6 fragments designated K–O; Two-color: grey-brown, black

136 Nine Memories, May, 1961; Tamarind No. 154; 22×30, bleed image; Edition: 8; Printer: Bohuslav Horak; Five-color: light greyish yellow, transparent yellow ochre, light blue, greyish green, sanguine

137 The Orator, June 8, 1961; Tamarind No. 305; 22×30, bleed image; Edition: 20; Printer: Bohuslav Horak

*138 Tenth Memory, August 24, 1961; Tamarind No. 365; 30×22¹/₄, bleed image; Edition: 25; Printer: Bohuslav Horak (Illus. p. 67)

139 Twelfth Memory, October 19, 1961; Tamarind No. 317; 30×22¹/₄, bleed image; Edition: 20; Printer: Bohuslav Horak; Four-color: yellow, violet, sanguine, green

140 Second Hero, November 14, 1962; Tamarind No. 658; 30×22¹/₄, bleed image; Edition: 8. Printer: Irwin Hollander; Two-color: black, pinkish white

141 Dead Center I, November 6, 1963; Tamarind No. 913 A; 30×22, bleed image; Edition: 10; Printer: Irwin Hollander

Color State:

Dead Center II; Tamarind No. 913; Edition: 20; Two-color: black, transparent grey

142 First Key, November 8, 1963; Tamarind No. 916 A; 19¹/₂ ×15, bleed image; Edition: 10; Printer: Jason Leese

Color State:

Green Key, December 30, 1963; Tamarind No. 916; Edition: 20; Two-color: green, blue

143 Walk on the Rocks, November 21, 1963; Tamarind No. 935 A; 30×22, bleed image; Edition: 9; Printer: Jason Leese

144 Three Observers, January 14, 1964; Tamarind No. 935; 30×22, bleed image; Edition: 20; Printer: Aris Koutroulis; Four-color: tan, blue, sepia, brown

145 Last Conversation, July 25, 1964; Tamarind No. 657; 29×19, bleed image; Edition: 20; Printer: Irwin Hollander; Three-color: black, ochre, white

146 At Last a Thousand I, October 4, 1965; Tamarind No. 1000-A; 24×34, bleed image; Edition: 10; Printer: Jurgen Fischer

* At Last a Thousand II, October 12, 1965; Tamarind No. 1000-B; Edition: 20; Four-color: blue, orange, light green, black (Illus. p. 69)

* At Last a Thousand III, October 15, 1965; Tamarind No. 1000-C; Edition: 10 (Illus. p. 70)

* At Last a Thousand IV, October 18, 1965; Tamarind No. 1000-D; 24×29, bleed image; Edition: 15 (Illus. p. 70)

147 Two Thousand Too Soon, April 3, 1967; Tamarind No. 2000; 30¹/₂×19, bleed image; Edition: 20; Printer: Fred Genis; Four-color: yellow-orange, green, transparent red, red

*148 Lemmings Crush, May 8, 1967; Tamarind No. 2001; 21× 30, bleed image; Edition: 20; Printer: Fred Genis; Seven-color: yellow, green, purple, orange, dull red, green, blue (Illus. p. 66)

*149 Stone Circle, May 15, 1967; Tamarind No. 2002; 24× 18¹/₂, bleed image; Edition: 16; Printer: Don Kelley; Five-color: grey-green, black, yellow, brown, purple (Illus. p.72)

*150 The Shelf, September 27, 1967; Tamarind No. 2003; 18^1/$_2$ × 24, bleed image; Edition: 25; Printer: Maurice Sanchez (Illus. p. 71)

151 Thirteenth Memory, September 29, 1968; Tamarind No. 2003, State II; 24 × 18^1/$_2$, bleed image; Edition: 7. Printer: Maurice Sanchez; Four-color: grey, white, yellow, brown

*152 To Get to the Other Side, January 29, 1968; Tamarind No. 2171; 16 × 16^1/$_2$, bleed image; Edition: 25; Printer: Maurice Sanchez; Two-color: red-black, black (Illus. p. 74)

153 Plus ça Change – –, March 7, 1968; Tamarind No. 2197, State II; 23 × 29^1/$_4$, bleed image; Edition: 25; Printer: Serge Lozingot

154 Lemmings Twenty-One, March 11, 1968; Tamarind No. 2197-MS; 22 × 28, bleed image; Edition: 4. Printer: Maurice Sanchez; Two-color: two blacks

155 Plus ça Reste … même, March 21, 1968; Tamarind No. 2197-SL; 22 × 28, bleed image; Edition: 20; Printer: Serge Lozingot; Three-color: green, blue, black

*156 Lemmings Day, March 26, 1968; Tamarind No. 2195; 20^1/$_2$ × 28, bleed image; 7 proofs; Printer: David Folkman; Two-color: two blacks (Illus. p. 73)

*157 Lemmings Night, March 26, 1968; Tamarind No. 2238; 21^3/$_4$ × 28, bleed image; Edition: 20; Printer: Serge Lozingot; Three-color: light brown, grey, black (Illus. p. 74/75)

158 Lemmings Choice, September 18, 1968; Tamarind No. 2003, State III; 26 × 19^1/$_2$, bleed image; Edition: 20; Printer: Maurice Sanchez; Seven-color: yellow, three rose-reds, two greens, orange

ETCHINGS

The etchings were executed in 1957–58. Dimensions of the plate mark are given in inches, height before width.

159 First Etching, 1957; 4^7/$_8$ × 7^7/$_8$; Edition: 3

160–163; Donne Series

160 "Two graves –," 1957; 6 × 11^7/$_8$; Edition: 10

161 The Baite, 1958; 11^7/$_8$ × 17^1/$_2$; Edition: 15

162 "Each hath one," 1958; 11^{15}/$_{16}$ × 8^3/$_4$; Edition: 15

163 "One room, an everywhere–," 1958; 14^1/$_2$ × 11^7/$_8$; Edition: 15
Note: Salt grains to produce surface embossing. Random sprinkling of these grains before each printing produced different embossed patterns on each etching.

164 Promenade, 1958; 11^3/$_4$ × 8^3/$_4$; Edition: 12
Note: Embossing, see note for no. 163

165 The Screen, 1958; 14^1/$_2$ × 11^7/$_8$; Edition: 5

166 The Unfinished Etching, 1958; 11^5/$_8$ × 17^3/$_4$; 4 proofs

MONOTYPES

167 "All day the same–," 1958; Donne Series; 11^3/$_4$ × 9. A series of fourteen unique color impressions (see text note 33)

EXHIBITIONS

ONE-MAN EXHIBITIONS

* illustrated catalogue/folder published

1935 Boulevard Gallery, Diana Court, Chicago, Illinois
1936 Palacio de Bellas Artes, Mexico City, Mexico, D.F.*
1950 Santa Barbara Museum of Art, Santa Barbara, California*
San Francisco Museum of Art, Civic Center, San Francisco, California
1952–1953 Pasadena Art Museum, Pasadena, California*
1953 Santa Barbara Museum of Art, Santa Barbara, California
The Contemporaries, 959 Madison Avenue, New York, New York*
1954 The Art Center of La Jolla, La Jolla, California
1956 M. H. de Young Museum of Art, San Francisco, California*
1958 The Achenbach Foundation for Graphic Arts, California Palace of the Legion of Honor, San Francisco, California*
Santa Barbara Museum of Art, Santa Barbara, California
1959 Los Angeles County Museum, Los Angeles, California, and Long Beach Museum of Art, Long Beach, California*
The Philadelphia Art Alliance, Philadelphia, Pennsylvania
1968 University of New Mexico, Art Museum, Albuquerque, New Mexico*

SELECTED GROUP EXHIBITIONS

Note: From over 230 national and international group shows in which the artist has participated between 1935 and 1968, the following exhibitions are listed because of their importance to the artist, or because a catalogue/folder was published for them with illustrations of the artist's work and/or extended details of her participation in the show. The asterisks indicate that a catalogue/folder was published.

1950 Los Angeles County Museum, Los Angeles, California. "Artists of Los Angeles and Vicinity"
1951 University of Illinois, College of Fine and Applied Arts, Urbana, Illinois. "Exhibition of Contemporary American Painting"*
Colorado Springs Fine Arts Center, Colorado Springs, Colorado. "13th Annual Artists West of the Mississippi Exhibition"*
Los Angeles County Museum, Los Angeles, California. "Contemporary Painting in the United States"*
The Art Institute of Chicago, Chicago, Illinois; "60th Annual American Exhibition of Painting and Sculpture"*
1952 The Art Institute of Chicago, Chicago, Illinois. "Lithographs by June Wayne, Etchings by Ynez Johnston"
California Palace of The Legion of Honor, San Francisco, California. "5th Annual Exhibition of Contemporary American Painting"*
1953 University of Illinois, College of Fine and Applied Arts, Urbana, Illinois. "Exhibition of Contemporary American Painting and Sculpture"*
1954 University of Illinois, Urbana, Illinois. "Graphic Arts, U.S.A."*
1955 Musée National d'Arte Moderne, Paris, France. "Salute to France"
Galeria Ibeu, São Paulo, Brazil. "Exposição Norte Americana da III Bienal de São Paulo"
The Whitney Museum of American Art, New York. "Annual Exhibition of Contemporary American Painting"
1956 Cabinet des Estampes, Chateau des Rohan, Strasbourg, France. "Dessins Americains Contemporaines"*
The Tate Gallery, London, England. "Modern Art in the United States"*
1957 The Grunwald Foundation of Graphic Art University of California at Los Angeles. "An Exhibition of Master Prints"
Colorado Springs Fine Arts Center, Colorado Springs,

Colorado. "16th Annual Exhibition of Artists West of the Mississippi"*

1957– Smithsonian Institution, Washington, D.C. "40 Paint-
1958 ers Circulated to 20 Museums"*

National Gallery of Art, Washington, D.C. "The Fantastic, Bizarre and Occult in Art"

1959 Print Council of America. "American Prints Today"*

Pasadena Art Museum, Pasadena, California. "1949–59,
A Decade in the Contemporary Galleries"*

Marion Koogler McNay Art Institute, San Antonio,
Texas. "Lithographs by June Wayne, Woodblocks by
Antonio Frasconi"

Musée National d'Art Moderne, Paris, France. "La
Jeune Gravure Contemporaine"

1960 Pasadena Art Museum, Pasadena, California. "2nd National Print Exhibition"*

Museo de Bellas Artes, Caracas, Venezuela. "75 Grava-
dores Norte-Americanos"*

1961 Japan Print Association, Tokyo, Japan. "29th Exhibition"*

1962 Otis Art Institute, Los Angeles, California. "Award
Winners 1953–1962"*

Grunwald Graphic Arts Foundation, University of California, Los Angeles, California. "Lithographs from the
Tamarind Workshop"*

1964 Smithsonian Institution, Washington, D.C. "The Fab-
ulous Decade, Prints of the 1950's from the Collection
of The Free Library of Philadelphia"*

Fine Arts Gallery, California State College at Fuller-
ton, Fullerton, California. "Four Women Artists–Elise
Cavanna, Claire Falkenstein, Dextra Frankel, June
Wayne"*

1965 Long Beach Museum of Art, Long Beach, California.
"Arts of Southern California, XVI: Prints"*

San Francisco Art Institute Gallery, San Francisco, California. "California Printmakers"*

1968 Cincinnati Art Museum, Cincinnati, Ohio. "American
Graphic Workshops; 1968"*

UNITED STATES

Achenbach Foundation for the Graphic Arts, California Palace of the Legion of Honor, San Francisco, California
Allen Art Museum, Oberlin College, Oberlin, Ohio
Amon Carter Museum of Western Art, Fort Worth, Texas
Art Center of La Jolla, La Jolla, California
The Art Institute, Chicago, Illinois
California State Colleges' Collection, Los Angeles, California
Cincinnati Art Museum, Cincinnati, Ohio
The Clark Library, Los Angeles, California
Columbia Museum of Art, Columbia, South Carolina
DePauw University, Greencastle, Indiana
The Grunwald Graphic Arts Foundation, University of California at Los Angeles, Los Angeles, California
The Houghton Library, Cambridge, Massachusetts
Iowa State University Library, Iowa City, Iowa
La Jolla Museum of Art, La Jolla, California
Lehigh University, Bethlehem, Pennsylvania
Library of Congress, Washington, D.C.
Long Beach Museum of Art, Long Beach, California
Los Angeles County Museum of Art, Los Angeles, California
Museum of Modern Art, New York, New York
The National Gallery of Art, Lessing J. Rosenwald Collection, Washington, D.C.
Newberry Library, Chicago, Illinois
New York Public Library, New York, New York
Northwestern University Library, Chicago, Illinois
Pasadena Art Museum, Pasadena, California
Philadelphia Museum of Art, Philadelphia, Pennsylvania
Philadelphia Print Club, Philadelphia, Pennsylvania
San Diego Fine Arts Gallery, San Diego, California
San José State College, San José, California
Santa Barbara Museum of Art, Santa Barbara, California
Smithsonian Institution, Washington, D.C.
University of California at Santa Barbara, Goleta, California
University of Minnesota Library, Minneapolis, Minnesota
University of New Mexico, Albuquerque, New Mexico
Walker Art Center, Minneapolis, Minnesota
Wilkie Foundation, Des Plaines, Illinois

FOREIGN

Bibliothèque Royale de Belgique, Brussels, Belgium
Bibliothèque Nationale de France, Paris, France

SELECTED BIBLIOGRAPHY

Books and Periodicals

"Art/A Dreamer's Intuitive View," *Fortnight,* December 22, 1952, p. 28 (illus., *The Lawcourt,* ptg.).

Art News, XLIX, January, 1951, p. 51 (illus., *Fireworks,* ptg.).

Art News, XLIX, February, 1951, p. 64 (illus., *Retreat,* litho.).

Arts and Architecture, drawings for covers, February, 1951 and February, 1953.

"Because Water Hates Grease," *Time,* LXXXIII, April 10, 1964, pp. 82, 85 (p. 83, illus., *Dorothy the Last Day,* color litho.).

Brooklyn Museum Bulletin, XIV, no. 1, 1952, p. 19 (illus., *Target,* litho.).

"Exhibition at Chicago's Art Institute," *Art Digest,* XXVI, May 15, 1952, p. 11 (illus., *Cavern,* litho.).

"Exhibition at Los Angeles," *Art News,* L, December, 1951, p. 63.

"Exhibition at Santa Barbara," *Art Digest,* XXIX, February 15, 1954, p. 29.

"Exhibition at the Pasadena Art Institute," *Art News,* LI, December, 1952, p. 41 (illus., *Study for the Bride,* drawing).

"Exhibition, Contemporaries Gallery," *Art Digest,* XXVII, March 15, 1953, p. 21 ff.

"Exhibition, Contemporaries Gallery," *Art News,* LII, April, 1953, p. 41.

"Exhibition of Oils, Drawings and Lithographs at the Art Center at La Jolla," *Art News,* LII, February, 1954, p. 50 (illus., *Curious,* litho.).

"Exhibition of Oils, Prints and Constructions at the Santa Barbara Museum," *Art News,* XLIX, March, 1950, p. 51 (illus., *Hero,* litho.).

"Exhibition of Paintings, Drawings and Lithographs at the Pasadena Art Institute," *Art Digest,* XXVII, December 15, 1952, p. 14.

Grafton, Samuel. "Tamarind: Where Artist and Craftsman Meet," *Lithopinion,* II, no. 1, issue 5, First quarter, 1967, pp. 18–25.

"Graphics at the Los Angeles County Museum," *Art News,* LVIII, April, 1959, p. 48.

Gray, Cleve. "Tamarind Workshop," *Art in America,* LI, October, 1963, pp. 99–100.

Heller, Jules. *Printmaking Today.* New York, 1958, p. 47 (Fig. 1–31, illus., *The Witnesses,* litho.).

Hofer, Philip. *The Artist and the Book, 1860–1960.* Catalogue by Eleanor M. Garvey. Boston, 1961, pp. 216, 218 (p. 218, no. 320, illus., *Song,* color litho.).

Informations et Documents, LV, October 15, 1956, p. 35 (illus., *Last Chance,* Fable Series, litho.).

"June Wayne to Exhibit Etchings," *Philadelphia Art Alliance Bulletin,* XXXVIII, no. 2, November, 1959, pp. 12–13 (illus. "She is all states," from *The Sunne Rising,* litho.).

Langsner, Jules. "Creative Pursuit, June Wayne," *Arts and Architecture,* LXVII, March, 1950, p. 30 (illus., *Chase, Cryptic Creatures, Tunnel,* ptgs.).

Langsner, Jules. "Imagist," *Arts and Architecture,* LXXIII, August, 1956, pp. 12–13 (illus., *Advocate, Bride, Messenger, Suitor,* ptgs.; *Travelers,* litho.; detail of *Bride,* litho. on cover).

Langsner, Jules. "Is There an American Print Revival? Tamarind Workshop," *Art News,* LX, January, 1962, pp. 34–35 ff.

Langsner, Jules. "Painting and Sculpture: the Los Angeles Season," *Craft Horizon,* XXII, July, 1962, p. 41 (illus., *Tenth Memory,* litho.).

Los Angeles Museum of Art Bulletin, VI, no. 3, 1954, p. 25 (illus., *Advocate, Bride, Suitor,* litho. triptych).

"New Talent in the U.S.; with note by the artist," *Art in America,* XLV, March, 1957, pp. 42–43 (illus., *Travelers, Tower of Babel* A, lithos.).

Newsweek, LIV, October 12, 1959, p. 115 (illus., *Adam Waiting,* litho.).

Newsweek, LIV, November 2, 1959, p. 9 (illus., detail *Adam Waiting,* litho.).

Rodman, Selden. *Conversations with Artists.* New York, 1957, pp. 28–30, 224.

Rodman, Selden. *The Insiders, Rejection and Rediscovery of Man in the Arts of our Time.* Baton Rouge, 1960, pp. 109–111 (illus., pl. 63, "Whatever dyes was not mixt equally," from *The Good-Morrow,* drawing).

Schlundt, Verna. "June Wayne and the Renaissance of Lithography," *Designers West,* XIII, November, 1966, p. 19.

"The Art of Selling Art," prepared for the National Retail Merchants Association, New York, September 7–9, 1966.

"Brussels Conclusion," *Arts and Architecture*, LXXVI, January, 1959, p. 7 ff.

"Foundation Gamesmanship," prepared for Creative Arts: The Living Culture of California, a symposium sponsored by the California Arts Commission, San Francisco, May 21 and 22, 1966.

"Graphic Workshops: The Tamarind Lithography Workshop," *Artist's Proof*, Vol. II, no. 1, issue no. 3, Spring, 1962, pp. 44–46.

"New Careers in the Arts," a position paper based on a speech delivered before the National Council of Fine Arts Deans, San Francisco, October 15, 1966.

FILM

"The Look of a Lithographer," Los Angeles, Tamarind Production, 1968. Directed by Jules Engel; written by June Wayne; produced and filmed by Ivan Dryer; narrated by Mark Jordon. 16 mm; black and white; sound; 45 min. Available from Films Inc., 1144 Wilmette Avenue, Wilmette, Illinois.